PRACTICAL DISCOURSES

ON

REGENERATION.

BY

PHILIP DODDRIDGE, D.D

WITH A MEMOIR OF THE AUTHOR.

Philadelphia:

AMERICAN BAPTIST PUBLICATION SOCIETY,

118 ARCH STREET.

STEREOTYPED BY GEORGE CHARLES.

INTRODUCTION.

Practical Discourses on Regeneration are among the most vital wants of this age. Although for the last century much has been written on this great doctrine, nothing has fallen under our observation so popular, so plain, so scriptural, and so practical, as the following production of Dr. Doddridge.

These Discourses were prepared with great care by their excellent author, and delivered on Sabbath evenings to his own flock at Northampton; which embraced, let it be remembered, about forty young men, of his Academy, most of them candidates for the Christian Ministry. They attracted the attention of members of other congregations—"a great many such persons of different persuasions and communions making up a part of the auditory." They were attended with uncommon diligence to the last, and long before the series was finished, were earnestly requested for publication. The request grew more importunate at the close. Strangers from a distance joined in it, including several ministers—believing that what had proved so beneficial in the hearing, would be no less so in the reading, both at home and abroad. "I thought myself bound in duty," says Dr. Doddridge, "at length to comply; which I was the rather encouraged to do from the several instances in which I had reason to believe the Divine blessing had in some measure attended these sermons from the pulpit, *and had made them the means of producing and advancing the change they described and enforced.*"

This was in 1741. It was the period of the "Great Awakening" under the labors of Whitefield, Edwards, and others in this country, the effects of which were felt so powerfully at the time, in breaking up old systems of formalism, and inveterate habits of ungodliness; and which, with all its incidental excesses and evils, has been the main instrument in moulding the evangelical religion of this land, to this day. The impulse then given, the ideas then set forth, with the demonstration and power of the Spirit of God, are yet at work among us for good. It is well known that Drs. Watts and Doddridge shared in this impulse with a vital sympathy. They were in communication with Edwards for years. Northampton in old England and Northampton in New England, were centres of kindred ideas and feelings.

And what was the GREAT DOCTRINE, which above all others was made prominent in the preaching of that time of God's power? What was that fundamental and fruitful TRUTH, which, before unknown, or inoperative because misunderstood, or neglected, now shook society to its centre, and cleared away old and worthless foundations, in order to rear anew the Spiritual Temple of the Most High? What but this very Doctrine of REGENERATION, to the discussion of which the following pages are so wisely and yet so warmly devoted.

The same great TRUTH, which in the age

of Christ and his Apostles swept away the false hopes of hereditary profession—"the children of the flesh, these are not the children of God"—became again the Ruling Idea of the AGE OF REVIVAL. So testifies the historian of "The Great Awakening." Speaking of this period he says, "The history of religious opinions and practices shows, that the most important practical idea, which then received increased prominence and power, and has held its place ever since, was the idea of the New Birth." "This doctrine of the New Birth, as an ascertainable change, was not generally prevalent in any communion, when the revival commenced; it was urged as of fundamental importance by the leading promoters of the revival; it took strong hold of those whom the revival affected; it naturally led to such questions as the revival brought up, and caused to be discussed; its perversions grew into, or associated with such errors as the revival promoted; it was adapted to provoke such opposition, and in such quarters, as the revival provoked; and its caricatures would furnish such pictures of the revival as opposers drew."*

When it is said above that the doctrine of the new birth was not generally prevalent in any communion before the beginning of the Great Revival, we must understand that while held as a part of an orthodox creed, it was not generally preached, and consistently applied. In some communions, as, for instance, in the Church of Rome and in the Church of England, the doctrine of Baptismal Regeneration prevailed. In New England the scheme of church membership, called the "Half-Way Covenant," had been generally adopted, with an effect almost equally fatal. Men of sounder views in Congregational and Presbyterian churches—to say nothing of the Lutheran, and Dutch and German Reformed—found their evangelical teaching on this point unpalatable to those who had been trained to believe that by baptism in infancy they were brought into covenant with God. These and similar causes had

* THE GREAT AWAKENING. By Joseph Tracy, Boston, 1842, p. ix. Preface.

lulled conscience asleep as with stupefying opiates, and "the form of godliness" to a great extent had supplanted its "power."

The scriptural doctrine of the New Birth struck at the root of all these forms of error. It was mighty through God. It became the leading idea of the age. "YE MUST BE BORN AGAIN," flashed from every pulpit, and penetrated every heart.

This great idea must in like manner take possession of our age, or FORMALISM will return. It must breathe into our countrymen the breath of a new life, or we shall become like the dry bones in the Valley of Vision. It must be set forth in our pulpits with all possible scriptural plainness; guarded from all perversion, on the right hand and on the left; fortified at every point by the testimony of God; and pressed to its genuine and resistless applications. All this must be done before the Church of Christ can rise again in her original beauty and vigor, or spread to her predestined greatness and glory—as the joy of the whole earth.

J. N. B.

Philadelphia, Dec. 13, 1854.

Contents.

PRACTICAL DISCOURSES

ON

REGENERATION.

DISCOURSE I.

OF THE CHARACTER OF THE UNREGENERATE.

EPHES. ii. 1, 2.

And you hath he quickened, who were dead in trespasses and sins; wherein in time past ye walked according to the course of this world, according to the prince of the power of the air, the spirit that now worketh in the children of disobedience.

AMONG all the various trusts which men can repose in each other, hardly any appears to be more solemn and tremendous, than the direction of their sacred time, and especially of those hours which they spend in the exercise of public devotion. These seasons take up so small a part of our lives, when compared with that which the labors and recreations of them demand; and so much depends upon their being managed aright, that we, who are called to assist you in the employment and improvement of them, can hardly be too solicitous, that we discharge the trust, in a manner which we may answer to God and to you.

If this thought dwell upon the mind with due weight, it will have some sensible influence upon our discourses to you, as well as on the strain of those addresses which we present to the Throne of Grace in your name, and on your account. We shall not be over-anxious about the order of words, the elegance of expression, or the little graces of composition or delivery; but shall study to speak on the most important subjects, and to handle them with such gravity and seriousness, with such solemnity and spirit, as may, through the Divine blessing, be most likely to penetrate the hearts of our hearers; to awaken those that are entirely unconcerned about religion, and to animate and assist those, who, being already acquainted with it, desire to make continual advances—which will be the case of every truly good man.

It is my earnest prayer for myself, and for my brethren in the ministry of all denominations, that we may, in this respect, approve our wisdom and integrity to God, and *commend ourselves to the consciences of all men.* 2 Cor. iv. 9. It is our charge, as we shall answer it another day to *the God of the spirits of all flesh,* to use our prudent and zealous endeavors, to make men truly wise and good, virtuous and happy: but to this purpose, it is by no means sufficient to content ourselves, merely with attempting to reform the immoralities and irregularities of their lives, and to bring them to an external behavior, decent, honorable, and useful. An undertaking like this, while the inward temper is neglected, even when it may seem most effectual, will be but like painting the face of one who is ready to die, or laboring to repair a ruinous house, by plastering and adorning its walls, while its foundations are decayed. There is an awful passage in Ezekiel to this purpose, which I hope we shall often recollect; (Ezek. xiii. 10—14;) "Wo to the foolish prophets—because they have seduced my people, saying Peace, when there was no peace; and one built up a wall, and lo, others daubed it with untempered mortar: say unto them that daub it with untempered mortar, that it shall fall:—Thus saith the Lord God, I will even rend it with a stormy wind in my fury: and there shall be an overflowing shower in mine anger, and great hailstones in my fury to consume it: so will I break down the wall that ye have daubed with untempered mortar, and bring it down to the ground, so that the foundation thereof shall be discovered, and it shall fall, and ye shall be consumed in the midst thereof; and ye shall know that I am the Lord."

If there be any, in one body of Christians or another, that abet men's natural disposition to flatter themselves *in a way that is not good,* by encouraging them to hope for salvation, because they were baptized in their infancy; because they have diligently attended on public worship, or merely because they do nobody any harm, but are rather kind and helpful to others; or because their faith is orthodox, their transports of affection warm, or their assurance confident; I pray God to awaken them by the power of his grace, before they are consumed, with their hearers, in the ruins of their deceitful building.

Those of you who are my stated hearers can witness for me, that in this respect I have *delivered my own soul.* Ezek. xxxiii. 9. It has been the steady tenor of my doctrine among you, that our hope and confidence must be in Christ, and not in ourselves; and that, if we desire to be interested in the righteousness he has wrought out, and in the blessings he has purchased by his sacred blood, we must be experimentally acquainted with the work of God's renewing grace upon our souls, curing the inward distempers of our degenerate hearts, and transforming us into the image of his holiness. That is what we are taught in Scripture to call by the name of *Regeneration;* and considering how much the subject is neglected by some, and I fear I may add, misrepresented and disguised by others, I apprehend I shall profitably employ an evening hour for several succeeding Sabbaths, in giving a larger account than I have yet done, of the scripture doctrine on this important subject and its various parts.

It shall be my care, in the series of these discourses, as God shall enable me, to *speak the words of truth and soberness;* (Acts xxvi. 27;) and I entreat you to have recourse *to the law and to the testimony,* (Isa. viii. 20,) that ye may judge of the truth and weight of what I say. I desire not to be regarded any farther, than I produce evidence from reason and scripture; but so far as we are disregarded while we have the concurrent testimony of both, our hearers must see to it; and their danger will then be proportionable to the importance of those truths, which their negligence, or their prejudice, engage them either to reject, or to overlook.

The plan, on which I intend to proceed in the course of these lectures, is this: I will endeavor to describe the character of those whom we may properly call persons in an unregenerate state. I will describe the nature of that change, which may properly be called regeneration, or conversion. I will show at large the absolute necessity of this change, and the consequent misery of those that are strangers to it. I shall endeavor to prove the reality and necessity of the Divine influences on the mind, in the production of such a change. I shall describe some of those various methods, by which God is pleased to operate in the production of this holy and important work. I shall propose some advice to those who are already awakened, as to the method in which they are to seek renewing and converting grace. After which, I shall conclude these discourses with an *address* to those who have experienced this *happy change*, as to the manner in which they ought to be affected with such a series of sermons as this, and the improvement they should make of what they hear and what they have felt agreeable to it.

I should be peculiarly inexcusable, if I entered upon such a subject, without earnest and importunate prayers to the Fountain of light, grace, and holiness, that while you hear of this important doctrine, you may have that experimental knowledge of it, without which such discourses will indeed seem obscure and enthusiastical, according to the degree in which they are rational and spiritual. I shall only add that these lectures will take their rise from a variety of texts, which I shall not, according to my usual method, largely open and dilate upon, but only touch on them as so many mottoes to the respective sermons to which they are prefixed.

As I intend not philosophical essays, but plain, practical, and popular addresses, I shall begin,

First, With describing the CHARACTER OF THOSE WHOM WE MAY PROPERLY CALL UNCONVERTED AND UNREGENERATE PERSONS. It is absolutely necessary that I should do this, that you may respectively know your own personal concern in what is further to be laid before you in the process of these lectures.

Now you have the general character of such, in the words of my text; and a very sad one it is. They are represented, as *dead in trespasses and sins,* utterly indisposed both for the actions and enjoyments of the spiritual and divine life; as *walking according to the course of this world,* a sad intimation that it was the state of the generality of mankind; nay, *according to the prince of the power of the air,* that impure and wicked *spirit, who works,* or exerts his energy, *in the children of disobedience,* that is, in those who reject and despise the gospel; in which it is implied, and a dreadful implication it is, that the course and conduct of those, who reject the gospel, is according to the desire and instigation of the prince of darkness: they are going on as the devil himself would have them, and choose that path for themselves, which he chooses for them, as leading them to most certain and most aggravated ruin.

And who are these unhappy persons? Surely there must be some of them among us: for who can flatter himself, that in so numerous an assembly, the course of all is different from that of the world: and that all have happily triumphed over the artifices of that accursed spirit, who is, by God's righteous permission, become *its prince*, while it continues in its apostate state? I shall however think it a very happy point gained, if I could convince any of you, who are justly liable to that conviction, that *you are the men;* if I could, as it were, render visible to your eyes those subtile, yet strongly complicated chains, in which Satan is binding you, and by which he is drawing you on to eternal ruin; that you might *recover yourselves out of the snare of the devil, who are led captive by him at his will.*

I am now to describe the *character* of unregenerate men; but I cannot pretend to do it in all the variety of circumstances which may attend it.

I shall therefore mention only some particulars which are most important, and which most certainly demonstrate a person to be of that wretched number. There are a great variety of countenances in the human species; yet the principal features in all are the same, though their proportion and lineaments may differ: and I apprehend, the characters which I am now to lay down, will most of them suit every unregenerate person, though they may appear in various persons in different degrees and different instances. I shall chiefly lay down these characters in negatives, as I apprehend it is the safest way: and would only observe, what you may easily imagine, that I speak only of the adult; for I would cautiously avoid entangling this Discourse with what relates purely to the case of infants, lest *Satan should get an advantage over us*, and turn that into an occasion to amuse curiosity, which I humbly hope, under the influence of the Spirit of God, will be a means of awakening conviction, and of breaking that delusive peace, in which, like *the strong man armed*, he keeps his vassals, till the fatal hour come which is to complete their ruin.

To waive the formality of labored demonstrations in a case which admits of such easy evidence, I shall go upon this obvious principle in the whole of my reasoning: That to be *regenerate*, and to be *born of God*, are in scripture terms of the same import; and consequently, that whatever *temper* and *disposition* is in scripture declared to be *inconsistent* with the *character* of *a child of God*, must necessarily denominate a man *an unregenerate person*. And one would think this principle could hardly be disputed, since all that allow of regeneration at all, in a Christian sense, seem to understand by it, that change, whatever it is, by which a person is made *a child of God*, and by consequence *an heir of heaven*.

Now on this principle, you may take the marks of an unregenerate person in such particulars as these; and let those, whose conscience owns them, hear and tremble.

1. The soul that *never seriously inquired into its spiritual state*, is, beyond all doubt, an unregenerate soul.

The Apostle earnestly presses it upon the Christians to whom he wrote, that they should diligently *examine themselves whether they were in the faith;* (2 Cor. xiii. 5;) and he who has entirely neglected to do it, seems to express, not merely a forgetfulness of religion, but even a contempt of it too. Nevertheless, be it known unto you, Sirs, that an humble return to God, and a cordial dedication of soul to his service, is not so slight an act of a man's life, that it should pass without any observation in doing it, or any serious reflection on having done it. *Religion* is a deliberate thing; it brings a man seriously to *consider his ways*, that he may *turn his feet to God's commandments;* (Psal. cxix. 59;) to *search and try them*, that he may *turn again unto the Lord.* Lam. iii. 40. A good man is so impressed with the thoughts of God, and of eternity, that perhaps he is rather ready to be over anxiously afraid and suspicious, in a matter of so great importance: and therefore will review on the one hand, the plan of salvation that God has laid down in his word, and on the other, the correspondency to it that he may discover in his own soul; and if there are any of you that have never been thus employed, any that have never separated yourselves awhile from other employments, that you might *seek and intermeddle with this* Divine *wisdom*, (Prov. xviii. 1,) you are assuredly strangers to it. If there are any of you that have never studied God's word, to learn his will from thence; that have never attended to sermons, that you might try yourselves by them, and, if possible, carry home something of the chief of what you hear, to assist your retired, and more diligent inquiries; you may now come to a very quick conclusion, and before you leave this place, yea, before I proceed to any further particulars, you may set it down as the memorable beginning of these lectures, and of this discourse, "I am already proved to be an unregenerate creature: I am *in the gall of bitterness and in the bond of iniquity.*" Acts viii. 23. Nay, you may add, that there are perhaps thousands of those that are unregenerate sinners, who have not been so careless and so insensible as you. For, indeed, Sirs, a man may begin an examination, and start back from the prosecution of it, before it is brought to any important issue; or trying himself by false characters, he may come to a conclusion, which will be so much the more dangerous, as it has been the more deliberate. For the sake of such therefore, I add,

2. The soul that is *not deeply convinced of its guilt before God, and desirous to seek deliverance from it by the Lord Jesus Christ,* is still in an unregenerate state.

All the promises of God's paternal favor do certainly imply the promise of forgiveness; and you well know, that these are appropriated to such as humble themselves before God: and that humbling which is merely external, and implies no deep sense of inward guilt can pass for very little with that God, *who searches the heart, and tries the reins of the children of men.* Jer. xvii. 10.

The Scripture assures us, that *whosoever believes that Jesus is the Christ, is born of God;* (1 John v.

1;) and nothing can be more certain from the whole tenor of it, than that *he that believes not, shall be damned,* (Mark xvi. 16,) and surely a state of *damnation* is not, and cannot be, a state of *regeneration.* But what is this faith in Christ? Is it no more than a bare notional persuasion, that he is the Son of God? If this were all, the devils themselves *believe;* (Jam. ii. 19;) and many were the instances, in which you know that they confessed it, and *trembled* before him. You cannot then be ignorant, that the faith, to which the promises of salvation are made, is a faith, which *receives the Lord Jesus Christ in all his offices;* which trusts his atonement, as well as admits his revelation; and flies to him for righteousness and life. And how can that man seek *righteousness* from *Christ,* who is insensible to his own *guilt?* or how can he depend on him for *life,* who is not aware that he is under a sentence of *death* and *condemnation?*

But imagine not you are secure, because you acknowledge yourselves to be sinners. If that acknowledgment be slight and formal, it shows you are strangers to the operation of that Spirit, whose office it is to convince men *of sin.* John xvi. 8. If you have not been made sensible of the pollution of your hearts as well as the rebellion of your lives; if you have not received as it were a *sentence of death in yourselves,* and submitted to that sentence as righteous, though ever so dreadful; if you have not been made to *loathe and abhor yourselves, and to repent in dust and ashes;* (Job xliii. 5;) if you have not *laid your hand on your mouth,* (Mich. vii. 16,) and *your mouth in the dust,* (Lam. iii. 29,) *crying out, Unclean, unclean,* (Lev. xiii. 46,) and in this sense at least, adopted that pathetic complaint, *O wretched man that I am! who shall deliver me?* (Rom. vii. 24,) it is a certain sign, that *sin* still *reigns in your mortal bodies,* (Rom. vi. 12,) and is unto this day *bringing forth fruit unto death.* Rom. vii. 5.

3. The soul that is *unconcerned about the favor of God, and communion with him,* is still in an unregenerate state.

Common reason may tell you, that a soul destitute of the love of God, can never be the object of his complacential regards; and that it is impossible you should love him, while you are unconcerned about his favor, and habitually indifferent to converse with him. You believe there is a God; you acknowledge that he is the great benefactor of the whole world; you know your happiness depends upon his favor; you wish therefore that you may enjoy it; that is, you wish that some way or other you may be happy, rather than miserable. But let conscience say, whether you have ever felt, that *in his favor is life;* (Psal. xxx.

5;) whether you have ever known what it is to cry out with intenseness and ardor of soul, *Lord lift up the light of thy countenance upon me.* Psal. iv. 6. Alas, Sirs, had you been *sons, God* would have *sent the Spirit of his Son into your hearts;* (Gal. iv. 6;) and if this be not the sincere, if it be not the habitual language of your soul; if you do not thus earnestly desire to live under the manifestations of the divine love, and to be able to say, *truly our communion is with the Father, and with his Son Jesus Christ;* (1 John i. 3;) you are spiritually dead, and under the fatal influences of that *carnal mind, which,* being *enmity against God,* (Rom. viii. 7,) engages men to live contented *without God in the world,* (Eph. ii. 12,) so long as *their corn and their wine increase.* Psal. iv. 7. A heart, thus alienated from God, was never savingly turned to him, and can have no just reason to imagine itself the object of his paternal favor.

4. The soul that is *destitute of a sincere love to mankind,* has reason to consider itself as in an unregenerate state.

You may, perhaps, think it unnecessary to mention this; but the Apostle was undoubtedly a much better judge, and his own words suggest this particular to me: *Beloved, let us love one another: for love is of God; and every one that loveth, is born of God, and knoweth God; he that loveth not, knoweth not God,* and consequently cannot be born of him; *for God is love.* 1 John iv. 7, 8. And our Lord strongly intimates the same thought, when he exhorts his disciples to the most universal and unlimited benevolence by this argument, *that ye may be the children of your Father which is in heaven;* (Matt. v. 45;) plainly implying, that otherwise they could not really be born of God, or claim him for their Father. Regeneration is to form a man for intimate communion with *the general assembly and church of the first born,* (Heb. xii. 23,) and to prepare him for the region of complete and everlasting love; and the first fruits of it are to appear, and to be manifested here. *It is a faithful saying, that they who believe in God should be careful to maintain good works;* (Tit. iii. 8;) and unfeigned love is to be the root of them; so that if you cannot stand this trial, your religious hopes are all delusive and vain.

Let me entreat you therefore, that you would now look into your lives and hearts. Do any of the malignant passions harbor there? Ask yourselves, "Is there any of my fellow-creatures, whom I wish to see miserable; or would make so, if it were in my power to do it by the secret act of my will, so that no mortal on earth should ever know me to be the cause of the calamity?" If it be so, and this be your settled temper, *you hate your brethren* and *are murderers;* (1 John iii. 15;) and therefore *are the children of the devil, who was a murderer from the beginning;* and we may thus say of you in the very words of our Lord, who never uttered a rash censure: *You are of your father the devil,* for his passions you cherish, *and his lust you would do.* John viii. 44.

But reflect farther, If you wish others no harm, do you really wish them well? and that so really, and so sincerely, as to be ready to do them good? For merely *to say unto them, depart in peace, be warmed and filled,* (Jam. ii. 16,) when you have it in your power to help them, is at once to *mock the poor,* and to *despise him that made him.* Prov. xvii. 5. You that are conscious of a mean selfish temper, and wrap yourselves up, as it were, in your own separate interests, or in those of your own families, and can feel a concern for no others; you that devise what you may imagine shrewd and prudent things, but none that are liberal and compassionate; you whose eye does not affect your heart, when you see the distresses of your brethren, while you *have this world's good, how dwelleth the love of God in you?* 1 John iii. 17. How can you imagine you are the children of him, whom you so little resemble?

Nay, permit me to add once more upon this,

that if all your compassion is only moved by men's temporal calamities, and works not in any degree with respect to their spiritual and eternal interests, you have reason to fear, that it is no better than an unsanctified humanity; and indeed, that you never have learnt the worth of your own souls, while you set so little value on the souls of others, even of those, to whom you profess and intend friendship. And this concluding hint is of importance to prevent a dangerous mistake, in which too many good natured sinners are ready to flatter themselves, and in which, perhaps, others are too ready to join in flattering them.

5. He that does not know what it is, to *struggle with indwelling sin, and heartily to resolve against indulging it in any kind or degree*, is undoubtedly still in an unregenerate state.

You will observe, I do not say, that every one who knows what it is, to feel a struggle in his own mind, when assaulted by temptations to sin, is a truly good man: the contrary is dreadfully apparent. A principle of natural conscience often makes very strong remonstrances against sin, and sends out bitter cries when subjected to its violence; and this is so far from denominating a man a real Christian, that it rather illustrates the power of sin, and aggravates its guilt. But when a man's inclinations run entirely one way, and when he gives a swing to his natural passions without any guard or restraint; when he is a stranger to any inward conflict with himself, and any victory over his own lusts, and his corrupted will; it is a certain sign, he is yet under the dominion of Satan, and is to be numbered among the tamest of his slaves. For *they that are Christ's have crucified the flesh, with the affections and lusts;* (Gal. v. 24;) have learnt to *deny themselves,* (Matt. xvi. 24,) and to *mortify their members upon the earth.* Col. iii. 5.

It is also of great importance to add, that there must be a resolution to oppose sin in every kind, and in every degree; for *he that is born of God sinneth not;* (1 John v. 18;) nay, it is elsewhere said, *He cannot commit sin;* (1 John iii. 9;) and though it is too visibly true in fact, and apparent from several other passages in the very Epistle whence these words are taken, that this expression is to be interpreted with some limitation; yet the least that it can be imagined to signify is this, that he does not wilfully allow himself in the practice of any sin. He has learnt to *hate every false way,* and to *esteem all God's precepts, concerning all things to be right;* (Psal. cxix. 128;) so that upon the whole, *if he might have his request, and God would grant him the thing that he longs for,* (Job vi. 3,) it would be this, to sin no more, and get rid of every sentiment, desire, and affection, in any degree contrary to the purity of God's nature and law. If, therefore, there be any of you, *that spare one accursed thing*, though you should seem eager on destroying all the rest—if it be the secret language of your soul, " There is but one lust that I will indulge; there is but one temptation that I will comply with;" I perceive *your hearts are not right in the sight of God;* (Acts viii. 21;) for though you could according to your pretended purpose, *keep all* the rest of *the law, and yet offend* in this *one point* alone, you would, in effect, be *a transgressor of all.* Jam. ii. 10. In short, *He that commitetth sin is of the devil;* (1 John iii. 8;) but *he that is begotten of God, keepeth himself, and that wicked one toucheth him not.* 1 John v. 18.

6. He that *does not know what it is, to overcome this world, and to place his happiness in another,* is yet in an unregenerate state.

This is another of those certain marks, which God has given us of his own children. *Whatsoever is born of God*—as it is very emphatically expressed in the original—*overcometh the world.* 1 John v. 4. (πᾶν τὸ γεγεννημένον ἐκ τȣ Θεȣ.) It is not, you see, the extraordinary attainment of a few more eminent Christians; but it is an essential branch of every good man's character;

for he is *begotten again unto a lively hope by the resurrection of Jesus Christ from the dead*, even *to* the hope of *an inheritance incorruptible, and undefiled, and that fadeth not away*. 1 Pet. i. 3, 4.

You have reason, therefore, to judge very sadly concerning your state, if you are strangers to this *lively hope ;* which is a very different thing from that *hope to be saved*, of which some people talk in so indolent, not to say in so profane a manner, as to show, that it is the *hope of the hypocrite*, which *will perish, when God takes away his soul.* Job viii. 13 ; xxvii. 3. If you are conscious to yourselves, that you *mind earthly things*, your *end* will be *destruction*, (Phil. iii. 19,) for having *your heart on earth*, it is plain *your* only *treasure is here ;* (Matt. vi. 21 ;) and if you govern yourselves by worldly maxims alone, and your great care be to obtain those riches and honors, which the children of the world pursue ; if the importance of eternity has never appeared in such a light, as to make you judge everything trifling that can come in competition with it ; nay, whatever your views of eternity have been, if you are not practically carrying on a scheme for it : and if you cannot, and do not, deny your worldly interest, when it cannot be secured without hazarding your eternal hopes ; it is plain you are *friends of the world*, in such a sense as none can be, but he must be *an enemy of God.* Jam. iv. 4. If indeed *you were dead* to the world, *and your life hid with Christ in God*, you would *set your affections on things above*, on those things which are there *where Christ sitteth on the right hand of God;* (Col. iii. 1, 2, 3;) but the want of this temper shows that you are *carnally minded, which it is death to be;* (Rom. viii. 6;) and that the redeeming love of Christ has never exerted its influence upon your souls, nor his cross had any due efficacy upon you; for if it had, *the world* would have been *crucified to you, and you to the world.* Gal. vi. 14.

7. The soul that *does not long for greater improvements in the divine life*, is still a stranger to the first principles of it.

You know, that we are *called*, as Christians, with *an high and holy calling;* (Phil. iii. 14; 2 Tim. i. 9;) and *as he* that is the author of this *calling is holy, so are we* to be *holy in all manner of conversation*, (1 Pet. i. 15,) and to be *perfect, even as our Father which is in heaven is perfect.* Matt. v. 48. Here will therefore be room for improvement, not only during our continuance in the present life, but through all the ages of a glorious eternity; and it is the ardent desire of every good man, that in this sense above all others, *his path may be like the shining light, that shineth more and more, until the perfect day.* Prov. iv. 18. And *this* is the *one thing* that he does, or that in which all his labors centre; being conscious to himself how *far* he is from *having already attained, or being already perfect, forgetting the things that are behind,* he *reacheth forth unto those things that are before,* and *presses toward the mark, for the prize of the high calling of God in Christ Jesus.* Phil. iii. 12–14. In this view he seriously considers the circumstances of life in which Providence has placed him; that he may observe the advantages, which these circumstances give him for religious improvements; and it is delightful to him to discover such advantages.

Now if there be any of you, who know nothing of this temper, you are certainly in an unregenerate state; for none can be born of God, that do not love him; and none can truly love him, that do not earnestly desire, more and more to resemble him. So that if your hearts can indulge such a thought as this, "I wish I knew how much religion would be just sufficient to save me, and I would go so far, and stop there;" your conscience must tell you that you secretly *hate religion,* and are unwillingly dragged towards the form of it, by an unnatural and external violence—the fear of misery and ruin in neglecting it; and that you are not actuated by the free and liberal principle of a nature savingly renewed.

8. The soul that *does not know what it is, to live by faith in Christ, and in dependence on his Spirit*, is still in an unregenerate state.

We *are all the children of God, by faith in Christ Jesus*, (Gal. iii. 26,) if indeed we are so at all; and *he that is joined to the Lord*, in this sense, *is one spirit* with him. 1 Cor. vi. 17. But *if any man have not the Spirit of Christ, he is none of his*, (Rom. viii. 9,) for as *God has predestined us to the adoption of children, by Jesus Christ, to himself*, (Ephes. i. 5,) so *of his fullness* it is, that *all* believers do *receive, even grace for grace*, (John i. 16,) or an abundance and variety of grace, by virtue of their union with him, *who is the head: from whom the whole body being fitly joined together and strengthened by what every joint supplies, by an energy proportionable to every part, increases to the edifying of itself in love.* Eph. iv. 15, 18.

These things, as you see, are not only hinted in Scripture, but are copiously insisted upon, as very material points; and though I readily acknowledge, good men may apprehend and consider them very differently, and may express those apprehensions in different phrases; yet as experience makes it plain, that those souls generally flourish most, who have the most distinct conceptions of them, and the most habitual regard to them; so I think it is plain from these Scriptures, that there can be no religion at all, where there is a total insensibility of them.

If, therefore there are any of you, that apprehend it is *enthusiasm* to talk of the *assistances of the Spirit;* nay, I will add, if there are any of you, that do not earnestly desire *these assistances,* and do not seek them daily from the hand of Christ as the great covenant head of his people, you are, I fear, strangers to some of *the first principles of the oracles of God,* (Heb. v. 12,) and are *sensual, not having the Spirit.* Jude, verse 9. And though you may now and then form a hasty, and perhaps a warm resolution in religion, you will quickly, with *the* proud *youth* that are conceited of their own sufficiency, *faint and be weary,* and with *the young men* you *will utterly fail;* while *they* only *that wait upon the Lord, shall renew their strength, shall mount up as on eagles'. wings,* and, pressing on with an unwearied pace, according to the different degrees of vigor which the different parts of their course may require, *shall run and not be weary, and shall walk and not faint.* Isa. xl. 30, 31. In short, if you do not *thirst after the water of life,* that is, (as the Evangelist himself explains it,) *the spirit, which they that believe on Christ shall receive,* (John vii.

39,) however bountiful he is, he makes no promise to impart it to you; and if you never receive it, all your other sources of comfort will soon be dried up, and the miserable condition of the creature, that asked in vain for one drop of *water* to *cool his tormented tongue,* (Luke xvi. 24,) will certainly be yours.

Here I apprehend multitudes will miscarry, who have *made a fair show* in the eyes of men; and if you are condemned by this mark, I am sure you will not be acquitted by any of the preceding. For all the branches of a holy temper have such connection with this, and such a dependence upon it, that a man, who is destitute of this, can have only the semblance of the rest.

And thus, I have with all plainness and faithfulness, as in the sight of God, and sensible of my account to him, laid before you a variety of hints, by which I think you may safely and truly judge, whether you be, or be not, in an unregenerate state: and I shall now beg leave to conclude this Discourse with one plain inference from the whole, *viz:*

That BAPTISM IS NOT REGENERATION, in the scriptural and most important sense of the word.

To prove this as a corollary from the preceding Discourse, I shall only assume this most reasonable concession, with which you may remember I at first set out: that *regeneration*, and *being born of God*, signify the same thing. Now I have shown you from a variety of *scriptures*, under the former heads, that *every one* whom the Sacred Oracles represent *as born of God receiveth Christ, overcometh the world*, and *sinneth not*. But it is too plain, that these characters do not agree to every one that is baptized: and consequently it evidently follows, that every one who is baptized is not of course born of God, or regenerate; therefore, that baptism is not *scriptural regeneration.*

I think no mathematical demonstration plainer, and more certain than this conclusion; and therefore, whatever great and ancient names may be urged on the other side of the question, I shall rest the matter here, without leading you into the niceties of a controversy so easily decided.* I would only further observe, that they who most vigorously contend for the other *manner of speaking*, (for after all it is but a dispute about *a word*,) acknowledge expressly, that a man may be *saved without* what they call *regeneration*, and that he may *perish with it*. And though persons are taught to speak of their state, in consequence of baptism, in very high, and, I fear, dangerous terms; yet when wise and good men come to explain those terms, it evidently appears, that many

* See Postscript, at the end.

of whom they are used, are *so* in a state of salvation as to be daily obnoxious to damnation! so the children of God, as also to be the children of the devil! and so inheritors of the kingdom of heaven, as to be children of wrath, and on the brink of hell!

Where persons of real piety apprehend themselves under a necessity of using such phrases with respect to all that are *baptized,* we cannot blame them for endeavoring to bring down their signification as low as possible; but they will, I hope, excuse those who choose to speak, in what they apprehend to be a more scriptural, rational, and edifying language.

It was matter of conscience with me, to state the matter as you have heard. I do therefore earnestly entreat you, my dearly beloved, in the name of our Lord Jesus Christ, and for the sake of your own immortal souls, that you *deceive not yourselves with vain words;* but that where your eternal salvation is so plainly concerned, you bring the cause, the important cause, to an immediate trial. And if you are convinced, as I suppose many of you quickly may be, that you are at present *dead in trespasses and sins,* then let me beseech you to reflect on what the most transient survey of the Scriptures may teach you, as to the danger of such a case. For though it will be my business, in the process of these Discourses, more largely to represent it, when I come to speak of *the necessity of the new birth*, God only knows, whether your lives may be continued, till we advance so far in the subject: and where a case of this kind is in question, the delay of a week, or even of a day, may be inevitable and eternal ruin.

DISCOURSE II.

OF THE NATURE OF REGENERATION, AND PARTICULARLY OF THE CHANGE IT PRODUCES IN MEN'S APPREHENSIONS.

2 COR. v. 17

If any man be in Christ, he is a new creature; old things are passed away, behold all things are become new.

THE knowledge of our true state in religion, is at once a matter of so great importance, and so great difficulty that, in order to obtain it, it is necessary we should have *line upon line* and *precept upon precept.* The plain discourse, which you before heard, was intended to lead you into it; and I question not but I then said enough to convince many, that they were in an unregenerate condition. Nevertheless, as there are various approaches towards regeneration and conversion, which on the whole fall short of it; I think it very expedient now to give you, what I may properly enough call *the counterpart* of this view; which I shall, by Divine assistance, attempt from the words I have now been reading.

The Apostle, who wrote them, was transported to such a zeal for Christ, and for the souls of men, that some thought him *beside himself*, (verse 13,) and no doubt many would represent him as the greatest enthusiast upon the face of the earth. But as it was *a very small thing to him to be judged of man's judgment*, (1 Cor. iv. 3,) he calmly vindicates himself, by declaring that there was a cause for all this warmth, as the honor of God, and the Redeemer, and the eternal salvation of men, were so intimately concerned in the affair. *The love of Christ*, says he, *constrains us*, or, (as the word properly signifies,) *it bears us away with it*, like a mighty torrent, which we are not able to resist; *because we thus judge, that if one died for all, then were all dead*, under the sentence of God's righteous law—or they would not have needed such an atonement as the blood of his Son; *and* we farther judge, *that he died for all, that they who now live*, only in consequence of his dying love, *should not henceforth live unto themselves, but unto him that died for them.* 2 Cor. v. 14, 15. We therefore live to this Jesus; we consecrate our lives and labors to this purpose; and in consequence of it, *we henceforth know no man after the flesh*, that is, we do not regard our temporal interests, nor consider how we may most effectually obtain the favor and friendship of those who may be useful to us in life; *yea, though we have known Christ after the flesh,* or have expected a temporal Messiah, who should make our nation triumphant over the Gentiles, and enrich it with the spoils of other nations, *yet now henceforth we know him no more* under such a character. Verse 16. And in this respect the same temper will prevail in the heart of every real Christian; and *therefore,* i. e. in consequence of what was said before of the Redeemer's love, *if any man be in Christ,* if he be really one of his faithful servants, united to him by a lively faith, and in consequence of that union interested in his salvation, *he is a new creature:* his views and sentiments, his affections and pursuits, are so entirely changed, that he seems, as it were, to be come into a new world, and to be transformed quite into another person from what he formerly was; *old things are passed away,* and, *behold* the astonishing transformation! *all things are become new.* This is the thought that I am now to illustrate; and you cannot but see, how proper a foundation it will be for our Discourse on,

The *second general head* I proposed, which is, Particularly to describe the *nature* of that great *change,* which passes on every soul, that is truly *regenerate*, in the scriptural, and most important sense of the word.*

And here it may hardly seem necessary to tell you, that I do not mean to assert, that the substance of the soul, and its natural faculties, are in a strict and proper sense changed; a man might as reasonably assert from such a Scripture, that the former body was annihilated, and a new one produced; and common sense and decency will not allow us to imagine, that the Apostle meant anything of this nature, by the general terms he uses here. But the plain meaning is, that when a man becomes a real Christian, the whole temper and character of his mind is so changed, as to become different from that of the generality of mankind, and different frcm what it formerly was, while in an unenlightened and unrenewed state. It is *not* merely a little circumstantial alteration; it is not assuming a new name, professing new speculative opinions, or practising some new rites and forms; but it is becoming, as we frequently

* Some choose to call the change here described, *renovation* rather than *regeneration*. I have given my reasons, (in the Postscript,) why I use the words promiscuously: but I shall endeavor, through the whole of these Discourses, so to state the *nature* of this *change*, as to have no controversy with good men of any persuasion about anything but the *name* of it; concerning which, I hope, they will not contend with me, as I am sure I will not quarrel with them.

say, in our usual forms of speech, a different creature or a new man.

And thus the sacred writers express themselves in many other passages, which very happily serve to illustrate this. They, in particular, represent God as promising, with relation to this work; (Ezek. xxxvi. 26;) *a new heart will I give them, and a new spirit will I put within them; and I will take away the heart of stone,* that stubborn, obstinate, impenetrable disposition they once had, *and will give them an heart of flesh,* a tender, compliant temper, which shall incline them to submit to my will with humility, and to obey it with delight. And thus, when the apostle had exhorted the Ephesians, (Ephes. iv. 22–24,) *to put off, with respect to their former conversation, the old man, which is corrupt according to its deceitful lusts,* he adds, *And be renewed in the spirit of your mind, and put on the new man, which after God,* or in conformity to his image, *is created in righteousness and true holiness;* which is further illustrated by his important exhortation to the Romans. Rom. xii. 2. *Be not conformed to this world; but be ye transformed by the renewing of your mind.* And on the same principles, what in one place he calls *the new creature,* (Gal. vi. 15,) in another parallel place he expresses, by *faith that works by love,* (Gal. v. 6,) and by *keeping the com-*

mandments of God; (1 Cor. vii. 19;) for all these, as equivalent characters, he opposes to *circumcision and uncircumcision,* or the mere externals of a religious profession; declaring the utter insufficiency of the latter, and the absolute necessity of the former.

The general nature of this change may then be understood by an attentive consideration of such Scriptures as those mentioned above: which indeed contain what is most essential on this subject. But for the more complete illustration of the matter, I shall particularly show you, that where there is reason to speak of a man, as one of those who are in Christ Jesus, or who are truly regenerate, there will be new apprehensions—new affections—new resolutions—new labors—new enjoyments—and new hopes.

Perhaps there are few important branches of the Christian character, which may not be introduced as illustrating one or other of these remarks. The former of them is indeed the foundation of the rest; because, as religion is *a reasonable service,* all the change which is made in the *affections* and *resolutions,* in the *pursuits, enjoyments,* and *hopes* of a good man, arises from that different view, in which he is now taught to look on those objects, the nature of which is to direct his choice, to determine his conduct, and regulate his passions; it will therefore be the business of this Discourse to show you,

I. That wherever there is a real principle of regeneration, there will be *new apprehensions* of things.

When God created the natural world, he said, in the very beginning of his work, *Let there be light, and there was light.* Gen. i. 3. And thus he deals in this new creation, which raises the soul from a chaos, to such a beautiful, well-ordered, and well-furnished frame. *God,* says the Apostle, *who commanded the light to shine out of darkness, hath shined into our hearts, to give the light of the knowledge of the glory of God, in the face of Jesus Christ;* (2 Cor. iv. 6;) whereas before, *the understanding was darkened, being alienated from the life of God, through the ignorance that was in them, because of the blindness* or perverseness *of their hearts.* Ephes. iv. 18.

Now this illumination, of which I am speaking, does not so much refer to a speculative, as to a practical and heart-impressing knowledge. It is true, that when a man once comes to be in good earnest in religion, he generally arrives at a clearer and fuller knowledge, even of the doctrines of Christianity, than he had before: for he then sets himself to inquire with greater diligence, and to seek light of the great *Father of Lights* with greater earnestness; he gets clear of many evil affections, that put a corrupt bias upon his judgment; and he comes within the reach of those promises, *Then shall we know, if we follow on to know the Lord;* (Hos. vi. 3;) *and if any man will do his will, he shall know of the doctrine, whether it be of God.* John vii. 17.

Yet, I think, I may very properly say, that at various times, when our *judgment* of any object is the same, our *apprehensions* of it are very different. It is one thing, for instance, to believe that God is the omnipotent, all-wise, and all-gracious governor of the world; and another, and very different thing, to have the heart powerfully impressed with an apprehension of his ability and readiness to help us. I will, therefore, a little more particularly illustrate those respects, in which the apprehensions of such as are really regenerate, differ from those which they formerly had: and I hope you will do yourselves the justice to reflect, as we go along, how far you have ever felt these apprehensions which you hear me describe. I have a pleasing persuasion, that many of you have felt them, in a much livelier manner than they can be described. I would observe then to you, that a regenerate soul has new apprehensions of *God*—of *itself*—of *Christ*—of *eter-*

nity—and of *the way* and *method* that God has marked out for its being *happy* there.

1. A regenerate soul has *new apprehensions* of the blessed God.

There are very few who pretend so much as to *doubt* of the being of a God; and fewer yet, that will venture to *deny* it. And, even among those who have denied it, and disputed against it, some, by their own confession, have felt their hearts give them the lie, and upbraid them for using the powers of reason and speech against the Giver and Preserver of both. I persuade myself at least, there are none that hear me this day, who would not look upon a professed Atheist as a monster, unworthy to be a member of human society, and little to be trusted in any of its relations. Yet after all, while the being of the blessed God is warmly asserted, his nature is so little understood and considered, that there are thousands who may still properly be said to be *without God in the world*, (Eph. ii. 13,) or in practice and temper, though not in notion, to be Atheists in it. Wicked men therefore, in general, are described as those that *know not God;* (2 Thess. i. 2;) but where God has determined to glorify his mercy in the salvation of a sinner, he *shines into the heart*, for his blessed purpose, *to give the light of the knowledge of the glory of God.* 2 Cor. iv. 6.

And thus the glories of the Divine Being are known to the regenerate soul in such a manner, as they are not to the most acute metaphysician, or the sublimest philosopher, who is himself a stranger to the spiritual life.

The person of whom we now speak, has new apprehensions of the *spirituality* and *omnipresence* of *God*,—of his *majesty* and *purity*,—of his *power* and *patience*,—of his *goodness*,—and his *intimate access to men's spirits*, with the reality and importance of his *operations* upon them. Permit me a little to represent the views of each, both to direct your inquiries, and also to impress your minds, and my own, with truths in which we have all so intimate a concern.

The divine *spirituality and omnipresence* is apprehended by the good man in a peculiar manner. That there is some immaterial Being, and that matter is moved by his active power continually impressed upon it, according to stated laws, is indeed so plain a dictate of reason, that I question not but the thought influences the minds of some, who have not so much acquaintance with language as to be able properly to express it: but, alas! it easily passes through, as if no way important. It is quite a different thing to *feel*, as it were, the presence of an infinite, intelligent and all-observing Deity, actually surrounding us in all times and places: to say from the heart, *O Lord, thou hast searched me, and known me*, so that *thou understandeth my thoughts afar off: whither shall I go from thy spirit, or whither shall I flee from thy presence? Thou hast beset me behind and before, and laid thine hand upon me;* (Psal. cxxxix. 1–7;) to feel, as it were, the hand of God, which indeed we may feel, if we duly attend to it, in all the impressions made on our bodily senses, and on the powers of our mind;—to feel ourselves even now supported by it, and to argue from the constant support of his hand, the never-failing notice of his eye. He reads my present thoughts; he knows, even now, all the secrets of my soul, and has always known them; has always observed my conduct in even the minutest particular; and recorded, in permanent characters, the whole history of my life, and of my heart; of this depraved, sinful life, of this vain, this treacherous, this rebellious heart.

With this conception of the divine observance are closely and intimately connected new apprehensions of the *purity of God*, and of his infinite *majesty;* views which mutually assist and illustrate each other. The irreverence with which the generality of men behave in the presence of God, and the easiness with which they admit the slightest temptation to sin against him, plainly show what low notions they have of him; but God does, as it were, appear to the eye of a renewed mind, arrayed in his robes of light and majesty; so that he is ready to cry out, '*I have heard of thee by the hearing of the ear, but now mine eye seeth thee;* (Job xiii. 5;) I see the eternal, self-existent, self-sufficient God, who *sits upon the circle of the earth, and the inhabitants thereof are as grass-hoppers;* who *spreadeth out the heavens as a tent to dwell in,* and looks down on *the nations as the drop of a bucket, and counts them as the small dust of the balance.* Isa. xl. 15, 22. *Who would not fear before him? who would not tremble at his presence?* (Jer. v. 22,) who would not revere that God, *who is of purer eyes than to behold evil, and cannot look upon iniquity?* (Hab. i. 13,) *who cannot be tempted with evil,* (Jam. i. 13,) but must see it, and hate it, even in all its forms?'

And such too are the views it has of his *almighty power,* that the enlightened mind will further add, 'A God of almighty power, who could speak a whole world into ruin, as he spoke it into existence—who by one single thought, by one silent volition, could easily abase the proudest creature in the universe, must have it in his power to bring me in a moment to the dust of death, and to the flames of hell; to lay me as low in misery, and to hold me as long in it as he should please. This,

O my soul, this is the God, against whom such feeble worms as we are daily offending, and whom we madly presume to make our enemy.'

This gives the regenerate man a further sense of the *patience of God,* than ever he had before. Others may look round upon the world, and wonder there is so much penal evil in it; but the renewed soul wonders there is not a thousand times more. When he sees, how *the world lieth in wickedness;* (1 John v. 19;) when he observes, how poor, impotent mortals are, many of them perhaps, in words blaspheming the God of Heaven; many more of them, most presumptously violating all the plainest and most important precepts of his law; and most of the rest, living in a perpetual forgetfulness of him, as if he were not at all, or were not so considerable as to be any way worth their notice; such an one cannot but wonder, that the Almighty Majesty of Heaven does not in a moment make himself known by the *thunder of his power,* and confound all their madness and folly, by crushing the world, with its inhabitants, into ruin. He often sees the rising sun, and the descending rain, with astonishment that it should be sent down on such a world as ours.

He has also more affecting views than ever of the *Divine Goodness.* Most men speculatively believe it; and they take occasion, even from that belief, to affront it; but a good man views it at once as a delightful and a venerable thing: he *fears the Lord and his goodness;* (Hos. iii. 5;) and while it encourages him, guilty as he is, to repose himself upon it as his hope, it awakens a generous kind of confusion at the thought of ever having offended him, and fills his very soul with indignation at the thought of repeating such offences.

And once more, the regenerate man has quite different notions than before, of the *intimate access which God has to the spirits of men,* and his *power of operating upon them.* The greatest part of men indeed consider not, as they ought, how the whole material world perpetually depends upon a Divine agency, and is no other than one grand machine, on which the great artificer continually acts, to make it an instrument of mercy to his sensitive and intelligent creatures. But there are yet fewer, who seriously consider, how entirely *the hearts of men are in the hand of the Lord,* and how much depends on his influences upon them. Nevertheless, experience teaches the renewed soul, that *he is the God of the spirits of all flesh,* (Numb. xxviii. 16,) and he not only views, but manages them as he pleases. "Lord," does he say, "this spirit of mine is shaded with thick darkness, but thou canst illuminate it; it is diseased, but thou canst cure it; it is *unstable as water*, (Gen. xlix. 4,) and lighter than a feather, yet thou canst fix and establish it; and whatever thou wouldst have me to be, and to do, for thy glory, and mine own happiness, thou canst *work in me both to will and to perform it:* (Phil. ii. 13:) so that all I need, to the rectitude and felicity of my nature, is only this, that I may have more of thine inward, vital, operative presence." It is not easy to conceive, what efficacy this thought has, for the transformation of the soul. But again,

2. New apprehensions are connected with these sentiments in the regenerate soul, concerning *itself*, and its own state.

It is surprising to think, how many run through successive years in life, without ever turning the eye of the mind inward, that the soul may survey itself. I speak not of a philosophical survey of the faculties of the mind; which, though indeed in its place it be useful and entertaining, is no more necessary in its refinement to a well-ordered state, than skill in anatomy is to a healthful constitution: but I speak of those views of the mind, which are in the reach of all, how low soever their genius, or their education may have been.

As all true happiness is an internal thing,

wherever God intends to produce it in the heart of a revolted, corrupted creature, and such, alas! we all naturally are, he leads it into a view of itself; and shows it, if I may be allowed the expression, a mixture of *grandeur* and *misery*, that lies within; which yet the greatest part of mankind live and die without ever observing. "I am here," does the awakened creature say, "an intelligent being; far superior to this well-wrought frame of flesh and blood, which God has given me for a little while to command, and which I must quickly drop in the dust; I am made capable of determining my own choice, of directing my own actions, of judging concerning the importance of ends, and the propriety of means in subserviency to them; and while I see a vast variety of creatures in different forms beneath me, I see no rank of creatures above me, nothing nobler than man, here on earth, where I dwell. Yet I see man, in the midst of his glory, a feeble, dependent, mortal creature, who cannot possibly be his own end, nor can of himself alone, by any means command or ensure his own happiness. Everything tells me, that he is the creature of God; and that it is the greatest honor and felicity, to know, and practically to acknowledge himself to be so: everything tells me, that it is most reasonable, that God, who is the great Original of man, should also be the end of his being; but have I made him the end of mine? My soul, thou art conscious to thyself, thou hast lived in many instances *without him in the world.* Ephes. ii. 12. He has given thee, even in the system of thine own nature, and of the visible beings that are round about thee, compared with his providential interposition in the management of them, the intimations of his holy and righteous will; he has expressed these dictates far more plainly in his written word: and when thou comest to examine them, how art thou condemned by them! When thou comest to think of the spirituality and purity of his being, and his law, how shameful does thy temper, and thy life appear to have been! what an infinite disproportion is there between that, and its perfect rule!

"And whom, oh my soul, hast thou offended? whose law hast thou broken? whose grace hast thou despised? The law, the grace of that eternal God, of whom I have now been hearing; who is here present with me, who is even within me, and who sees, O my heart, more distinctly than thou canst see, all thy guilt, and all its aggravations. Oh Lord! *I abhor myself, and repent in dust and ashes.* Job xlii. 6. I have talked of sin, and of the sentence of God against it, as a thing of course: but oh, my soul, it is thine own concern! The guilt, the stain of sin is still upon thee; the sentence of God is pronounced against thee; and it must be reversed, or thou art undone forever! These irregular habits and dispositions that prevail in thee, must be corrected, or they will prove thy mortal disease, and everlasting torment. Thou art a poor, weak, irresolute creature; the experience of every past day of life, since I began to think of religion at all, proves it; yet thou must, by some means or other, attain to inward strength and inward purity, or thou art lost: and all these great capacities, and glorious faculties, will but make thy ruin so much the more distinguished. Oh how weighty the care! oh how great the charge! What shall I do, that *thought*, that *reason*, that *immortality*, may not be my destruction? Where shall I find a rock, that will be firm enough for my support and safety? Where shall I find the means, to build the fabric of such a happiness as thine, O my soul, must be, if ever I am happy at all?"

Thus does God teach the mind, by its inward reviews and reflections, this important lesson of its own impotence and guilt, of its depravity and ruin; and so prepares it for those new apprehensions of Christ, which I mentioned as the third particular.

3. The regenerate soul has new apprehensions concerning the *Lord Jesus Christ*, considered as

a Mediator in general, and as such a particular Mediator as he is exhibited in the word of God.

That affecting view which the regenerate soul has of the majesty, glory, power, and purity of the blessed God, will undoubtedly convince him how unfit he is in himself to appear before his awful presence. He is ready to sink down in the dust at the very thought, and to say, "*Who is able to stand before such a* great and *holy God*, as thou art? 1 Sam. vi. 20. If I were in all the original rectitude and glory of my nature, I could not do it: how much less, surrounded as I am, with so much guilt, with so much pollution! I need, as it were, *a daysman betwixt us, who might lay his hand upon us both*, (Job. ix. 33,) who should transact affairs in my name with God, and bring the peaceful messages of God to me: *let* such an one *speak with me and I will hear; but let not God speak with me, lest I die.*" Exod. xx. 19.

And when he comes to take a more near and intimate view of this Mediator which God has exhibited in the Gospel, the renewed soul is even charmed and transported with the view: and that Jesus, whose name he before pronounced with so much coldness, that the very mention of it was a kind of profanation, now is regarded by him as *the chiefest among ten thousand.* Cant. v. 10. He *beholds his glory*, as that *of the only begotten of the*

Father, full of grace and truth. John i. 14. The union of the divine and human nature in the person of Christ, though it appears indeed a mystery, which he cannot fully explain, is nevertheless a glorious certainty, which in the general, he most cordially believes. He sees *Emanuel—God* dwelling *with us* in human flesh, and acquiesces in the sight; while the rays of Divine Glory are attempered by passing *through the veil, that is to say, his flesh.* Heb. x. 20. He considers *Christ* as *made of God* unto him *wisdom, and righteousness, and sanctification, and redemption;* (1 Cor. i. 30:) and each of these views rejoices him to the very heart. "Ignorant as I am, I shall be taught and instructed by him, that great Prophet, whom God sent into the world; by him, who is incarnate wisdom, as well as incarnate love; whose words resound in the Gospel, and whose Spirit seals the instructions of his word. Guilty as I am, my crimes shall be expiated; for there is *redemption in his blood;* even *the forgiveness of sins;* (Eph. i. 7;) there is an *everlasting righteousness* that he has introduced: and oh, how richly will it adorn my soul! This pollution of mine shall not forever exclude me from a comfortable intercourse with the pure majesty of Heaven; for Christ is come to be my sanctification; and he can cleanse me by his Spirit, and transform me into that divine, delightful image which I have lost. Victorious Lord, how easily canst thou redeem me from that state of servitude, in which I have been kept so long complaining! How easily, and how powerfully, canst thou vindicate me *into the glorious liberty of the children of God!* Rom. viii. 21. Blessed Jesus, thou art my light and my strength, my hope and my joy! Thou art just such a Saviour as my necessity requires; thou fillest up all my wants, and all my wishes; thou art *all in all* to me! I would not be ignorant of thee for ten thousand worlds. I would not live a day, nor an hour, without recollecting who, and what thou art, and maintaining that intercourse with thee, which is the life of my soul."

4. The regenerate soul has also new apprehensions of the importance of *eternity*, when compared with time and all its concerns

It is indeed a most pitiable thing, and awakens our astonishment, grief, and indignation, to observe how the things of this world press down immortal spirits, and reduce them almost indeed to a state of brutality. Most deplorable it is, to see the power and energy of those motives, which are taken merely from this earth, and its little concernments, so that if a man did but know what was the *favorite vanity*, he might almost predict, from the knowledge of circumstances, how a man's actions would be ordered; and might almost be sure that he would follow, whithersoever this interest, or that pleasure, this ambitious, or that mercenary view, called him; though all the prospects for an eternal world pleaded the contrary way. Such is the *folly* and *madness* that *is in men's hearts while they live; and after that they go down to the dead,* (Eccles. ix. 3,) and spend that immortal duration, which they have despised, in fruitless lamentations. Fatal delusion! which it is the great design of the Gospel to cure.

But when a soul becomes *wise to salvation*, it is taught to *look not at the things which are seen, but at the things which are not seen; because* it has now a full sense of what before it only notionally confessed, that *the things which are seen, are temporal; but the things that are not seen, are eternal!* 2 Cor. iv. 18. ETERNITY! it is impossible I should tell you how much an eye, that is enlightened by God, sees, and reads, as it were, in that one word; while one scene beyond another is still opening on the mind, till its sight and its thoughts are swallowed up: and as the creatures are as nothing with respect to God, so all the interests of time, with respect to eternity, appear *as less than nothing and vanity.* Isa. xl. 17. To be made for an everlasting existence appears in so awful a view, that while it has some pleasing hope, it *rejoices with trembling;* and every remaining fear, with relation to this great interest, seems a greater evil, than the certainty of any temporal calamity.

I might add upon this head, that the regenerate soul has not only new views of the *importance*, but likewise of the *nature* of the invisible and eternal state; and particularly of the nature of the celestial happiness. It does not consider it merely, or chiefly, as a state of corporeal enjoyment, formed to gratify and delight the senses; but as a state of perfect conformity to God, and most endearing intercourse with him; of which, as it begins already by Divine Grace to taste the pleasures, so it most ardently thirsts after them; and would be heartily willing to lose this body forever, and to bid an eternal adieu to every object capable of giving it delight; rather than it would consent to lose, in a perpetual succession of such objects, the sight of the *Father of Spirits*, and that sensibility of his love, which adds the most substantial solidity, and exalted relish, to every inferior good that can be desired from it.

5. A regenerate man has also new apprehensions of *the way* which God has marked out *to this happiness.*

Nothing is more common than for carnal and ignorant men to imagine, that it is a very easy thing to get to Heaven; and upon this presumption, they *hew out to themselves cisterns, broken cisterns, that can hold no water;* (Jer. ii. 13;) and often live and die with *a lie in their right hand.* Isa. xliv. 20. But the renewed soul, having such awful conceptions of the blessed God, and such apprehensions of the excellency and glory of the heavenly state, as you have heard, deeply feels how absolutely necessary it is, that something of a very great and important *change* should pass in the mind of that sinful creature, that ever hopes to be a partaker of it. He sees, that it is impossible any external profession, or external rite, should secure so great an end—impossible, that *baptism* should be *regeneration,* in that sense in which the Scripture uses the word, or that by this alone, though ever so regularly administered, a man's eternal happiness should be secured. He sees, that to be associated to this or that party of Christians, to join with established, or with separate churches, and to be ever so zealous for their respective order, worship, and discipline, is a thing quite of foreign consideration here; and that the best, or the worst of men, may be, and probably are, on one side and on another; nay, that ignorance, pride, and bigotry may take occasion from hence to render men *farther from the kingdom of God,* than any mistake in judgment or practice, on these disputed points, could have set them.

No, my brethren, when a man's eyes are enlightened by God's renewing Spirit, he sees and feels that, in the language of Scripture, he must be *created* anew *in Christ Jesus;* (Ephes. ii. 10:) he sees, that *holiness* is a character *without which no man shall see the Lord;* (Heb. xii. 14;) and he is perhaps little anxious, whether *this,* or the *faith* that produces it, shall be called a condition, or a qualification, or an instrument, while he sees he must perish without it: he sees, that as it is absolutely necessary, so it is very extensive, *as the commandment,* which is its rule, *is exceeding broad:* (Psal. cxix. 96:) he sees, that it must not only effectually regulate the actions of his life, but control all the sentiments of his heart: nay, he sees it must not only be submitted to as a necessary, but be chosen as a most amiable thing: and, accordingly, he does choose it as such. The unregenerate soul, when he hears of repentance and reformation, though he understands not half that it means, nor is aware of what will, in fact, be the greatest difficulty of it, looks upon it at best as a nauseous medicine, which he must take, or die: but the regenerate man finds his heart so wonderfully and so happily changed, that he regards it for itself, as the food, the health, and the life of his soul; as that which necessarily brings its own pleasures, and, in a considerable degree, its own reward along with it; so that now, as David beautifully expresses it, *He openeth his mouth, and panteth, because he longs for God's commandments.* Verse 131.

And I will add once more, the good man is also made sensible of the place which faith and holiness hold, in the scheme which God has laid, for our justification before him, and our acceptance with him. I do not say that *all Christians* conceive of this with equal perspicuity, or express their conceptions with equal exactness: the most candid allowance should here be made for the different ideas they fix to the same phrases, as they have been used to look upon them with veneration, or with suspicion. But this I will venture to say, because I am persuaded the Scripture will bear me out in it—that the confidence of a regenerate soul is not fixed on his own holiness, or faith, as the meritorious cause of his acceptance with God. He is deeply and cordially sensible, that *he is made accepted in the Beloved;* (Ephes. i. 6;) and seeing nothing but guilt, and weakness, and ruin in himself, he ascribes to the blessed Jesus, and to the riches of God's free grace in him, his righteousness, his strength, and his salvation. And where a man is thus persuaded, I think he must, in effect, believe, even though he might scruple in words expressly to own it, "that Christ as our great Surety having perfectly obeyed the law of God himself, and by his blood having fully satisfied the Divine Justice for the breach of it, we, on our believing in him by a vital faith, are justified before God by the imputation of his perfect righteousness." This latter way of stating it, when rightly explained, appears just equivalent to the former; and it is a manner of conceiving and expressing it, which, when rightly understood, seems extremely suitable to that deep humility, and poverty of spirit, to which the renewed soul is brought, when, *like a new-born babe, it desires the sincere milk of the word, that it may grow thereby.* 1 Pet. ii. 2. But as the mind, at such a time, finds little inclination to contend about words and phrases, it would be much less proper for me, to enter into any controversy about them here.

Let it suffice for the present, that I have given you this plain representation of that change, which is wrought in a man's apprehensions, when he is made a new creature. *When old things are passed away*, he has *new apprehensions* of *God*, of *himself*, of *Christ*, of *eternity*, and of *the way* to obtain the *happiness* of it: and as at this happy time *all things are become new*, there are, "new affections, new resolutions, new labors, new enjoyments, and new hopes," which are the result of the change already described. But it will be much more difficult to reduce what I have to offer on these heads, within the bounds of the next Discourse, than proper to attempt any of them in this. Go home, my friends, and try yourselves by what you have already heard; and be assured, that if you are *condemned* by this part of the description, it is impossible you should be *approved* by any that will follow; since they have all their foundation in this.

DISCOURSE III.

OF THE NATURE OF REGENERATION, WITH RESPECT TO THE CHANGE IT PRODUCES IN MEN'S AFFECTIONS, RESOLUTIONS, LABORS, ENJOYMENTS AND HOPES.

2 Cor. v. 17.

If any man be in Christ, he is a new creature; old things are passed away, behold, all things are become new.

Among the various subjects, which exercise the thoughts and tongues of men, few are more talked of than *Religion.* But it is melancholy to think how little it is understood; and how much it is mistaken and misrepresented in the world.

The text before us gives us a very instructive view of it: such a view, that I am sure, an experimental knowledge of its sense would be infinitely preferable to the most critical and exact knowledge of all the most curious passages, both of the Old Testament, and the New. From it, you know, I have begun to describe that great change, which the word of God teaches us to represent under the notion of *regeneration,* or, according to the language of St. Paul, in this passage of his writings, by a *new creation*. I know I am explaining it to many, who have been much longer acquainted with it than myself; and it becomes me to believe, to many that have attained much higher advancement in it: but I fear also at the same time, I speak of it to many, who are yet strangers to it; and I am laboring, by the plainest addresses that I can, to give them at least some just ideas of it. Oh, that to all the descriptions that either have, or shall be given, God may, by his grace, add that understanding which arises from feeling correspondent impressions on the mind!

I have already endeavored to illustrate those new apprehensions, which arise in the regenerate mind; apprehensions of the blessed God, of itself, of Christ, of the eternal world, and of the way to obtain the happiness of it. It now remains, that I consider those "new affections, resolutions, labors, enjoyments, and hopes," which result from them. I observe, therefore,

II. That these *new apprehensions* will be attended with *new* AFFECTIONS.

I readily acknowledge, that the degree in which the affections operate, may, and will be different, in different persons, according to their natural constitution: but, as in some degree or another, they make an essential part of our frame, it is impossible but they must be impressed with a matter of such infinite importance, as religion will appear. And the apprehensions described above, must awaken the exercise of correspondent affections, and direct them to objects very different from those by which they were before excited, and on which they were fixed. And here now,

1. This may be especially illustrated in *love*.

Love is indeed the ruling passion of the mind, and has all the rest in an avowed and real subjection to it. And here lies the very root of human misery in our fallen and degenerate state: we are naturally *lovers of ourselves* in a very irregular degree—*lovers of pleasures, more than lovers of God.* 2 Tim. iii. 4. But, on the contrary, *the first and great commandment of the law* is written in the breast of every regenerate man: *thou shalt love the Lord thy God with all thine heart, and with all thy soul, and with all thy mind.* Matt. xxii. 37, 38. It is true, indeed, that if his soul were perfectly delivered into this mould, and his attainments in Divine love were complete, there would be an end of all sin, and almost of all calamity too: for what evil could assail or impress a mind entirely and unchangeably fixed upon God?

Yet that the love of God should be the prevailing affection, is not merely a circumstance, but an essential part of true religion. While the good man *sees Him who is invisible,* (Heb. xi. 26,) as infinitely perfect in himself, and as the author of being and happiness to the whole creation, he cannot but acknowledge, that he is, beyond comparison, the most amiable of all objects. And though it is certain, that nothing can so much induce and inflame our love to God, as a well-grounded assurance, that he is become our God, and our Father in Christ; yet before the regenerate soul has attained to this, a sense of those favors which he received from God in common with the whole human race, and more especially of those which are inseparable from a Christian community, together with the apprehension of his being accessible through the Mediator, and reconcilable to sinful men, will diffuse some delightful sense of God over the mind; which will grow sweeter in proportion to the degree in which his own hopes brighten and settle, while they are growing toward the *full assurance of faith.*

And as the real Christian *loves him that begat, he loves him also that is begotten of him.* 1 John v. 1. He *loves the Lord Jesus Christ in sincerity,* (Eph. vi. 24,) viewing him not in a cold and insensible manner, as he once did, but with inflamed affection, *as the chiefest among ten thousand, and altogether lovely.* Cant. v. 10, 16. If he *knows*, in any degree, *the grace of our Lord Jesus Christ*, (2 Cor. viii. 9,) in becoming incarnate for the salvation of his people, in making himself a sacrifice for their sins, and paying his life for the ransom of their lives; he feels himself *drawn* toward Jesus, thus *lifted up on the cross;* (John xii. 32;) *and the love of Christ constrains him*, (2 Cor. v. 14,) to such a degree, that he longs to find out some acceptable method to express his inward and overbearing sense of it. How divided soever true Christians may be in other respects, they all agree in this, in *loving* that *Jesus whom they have not seen.* 1 Pet. i. 8.

We may further recollect on this head, that the Apostle, in a solemn manner, adjures Christians *by the love of the Spirit;* (Rom. xv. 30;) thereby plainly implying, that such a love to him is an important branch of their character: and it must be so in all those who regard him, as every regenerate soul does, as the author of divine light and life, and as the source of love and happiness, by whom this *love of God is shed abroad in the heart*, (Rom. v. 5,) while it is *enlarged* with sacred delight to *run the way of his commandments:* (Psal. cxix. 32:) as that *Spirit*, by whom *we are sealed to the day of redemption*, (Eph. ix. 30,) and who brings down the foretastes of Heaven to the heart in which he dwells, and which, by his presence, he consecrates as *the temple of God.* 1 Cor. iii. 16.

And most natural is it, that a soul filled with these impressions and views should overflow with unutterable joy, and feeling itself thus happy in an intercourse with its God, should be enlarged in love to man: *for*, says the Apostle, *ye are taught of God to love one another.* 1 Thess. iv. 9. Those whom he apprehends as his brethren by regenerating grace, he knows are with him beloved of the Lord; and as he hopes to dwell with them for ever in glory, he must love them so far as he knows them now. And though a narrow education, and that bigotry, which sometimes conceals itself under very honorable and pious names, may perhaps influence even a sanctified heart, so far as to entertain unkind suspicions as to those, whose religious sentiments may differ from his own, and it may be, to pass some rash censures upon them; yet as his acquaintance with them increases, and he discerns, under their different forms, the traces of their common Father, his prejudices wear off, and that sometimes by very sensible degrees; and Christians *receive one another, as Christ has received* them all. Ro. xv. 7.

And where the good man cannot love others with a love of complacency and esteem, he at least beholds them with a love of compassion and pity; and remembers the relation of fellow-creatures, where he sees no reason to hope that they are *fellow-heirs* with him. In a word, the heart is melted down into tenderness; it is warmed with generous sentiments; it longs for opportunities of diffusing good of all kinds, both temporal and spiritual, wide as its influence can reach; it beats with an ardor, which sometimes painfully recoils upon a man's self, for want of ability to help others in proportion to his desire to do it; and that God, who knows all the inmost workings of his mind, hears many an importunate intercession for others in the hour of solemn devotion, and many a compassionate ejaculation, which he is occasionally sending up to Heaven from time to time, as he passes through so sinful and so calamitous a world.

These are the *ruling* affections in the heart of a good man; and though it is neither reasonable nor possible, that he should entirely divest himself of self-love, yet he endeavors to regulate it so, that it may not interfere with the more important consideration of general good. Self has the lowest place in his regards, nor does he limit his affection to a party; but aiming at extensive usefulness, he guards against those immoderate attachments to particular friendships, and those extravagant sallies of personal fondness, which are often no more than self-love under a specious disguise; which at once alienate the heart from God, and contract the social affections within very narrow, and those very irregular bounds; and so prove almost as fatal to the health of the mind, as an excessive flow of blood into one part would be to that of the body.

I have enlarged so copiously on this change in the leading affections of the mind, that I must touch in a more transient manner on the rest. I add, therefore,

2. That a regenerate soul has *new aversions.*

He once *hated knowledge, and did not choose the fear of the Lord.* Prov. i. 29. He *hated the light,* (John iii. 20,) which disclosed to the aching eye of his conscience the beloved and indulged irregularities of his heart. He hated everything that laid an embargo upon his lusts; and was ready to count those for his enemies that plainly admonished him, and secretly to dislike those whose conduct even silently reproved him. But now all these things are amiable to him; and those are esteemed his most valuable friends, whose example may be most edifying, whose instructions may be most useful, and whose admonitions may be most faithful. For he now *hates every false way;* (Psal. cxix. 104;) yea, and every *vain thought* too. Verse 113. He looks upon every irregular desire as an enemy, which he longs utterly to subdue; and especially strives against *that sin which does most easily beset him*, and abhors it more than he ever delighted in it. And though he rather pities than hates the persons of the most wretched and mischievous transgressors, yet he can no longer continue an endearing friendship with those, who were once his seducers to sin, and his companions in it. In this sense, like David, he *hates the congregation of evil-doers, and will not sit with the wicked;* (Psal. xxvi. 5;) and if they will not be wrought upon by his compassionate endeavors to reclaim them, he will soon break off the infectious intercourse, and say, *Depart from me ye evil-doers, for* I determine that *I will keep the commandments of my God.* Psal. cxix. 115.

3. The regenerate man has also *new desires.*

There was a time, when *sinful passions*, as the Apostle expresses it, *did work in his members to bring forth fruit unto death.* Rom. vii. 5. He was *fulfilling the desires of the flesh, and of the mind*, (Eph. ii. 3,) and *making provisions to fulfil the lusts* of both. Rom. xiii. 14. But now he earnestly desires a conformity to God, as his highest happiness; and can look up to him, and say, "*O Lord, the desire of my soul is to thy name, and to the remembrance of thee;* (Isa. xxvi. 8;) to maintain such a sense of thy presence at all times, as may influence my heart to think, my lips to speak, and my hands to act, in a manner suitable to that remembrance, and agreeable to thy wise and holy will." He now *hungers and thirsts after righteousness;* (Matt. v. 6;) feels as real an appetite after more advanced degrees of piety and holiness, as he ever felt toward the gratification of his senses; and esteems the proper methods of attaining these advanced degrees, even *more than his necessary food.* Job xxiii. 12. Instead of desiring to run through a long course of animal enjoyments, he desires to get above them; longs to be a pure and triumphant spirit in the refined regions of immortality; and *is willing rather to be absent from the body, and to be present with the Lord.* 2 Cor. v. 8.

But I waive the farther illustration of this, till I come to consider the new hopes which inspire him. I therefore add, as a necessary consequence of these new desires,

4. That the regenerate man has *new fears.*

Pain and sorrow, disappointment and affliction, he naturally feared; and the forebodings of his own mind would sometimes awaken the fears of future punishment, according to the righteous judgment of an offended God: but now he fears not merely punishment, but guilt; fears the remonstrance of an injured conscience; for he reverences conscience as God's vicegerent in his bosom. He therefore fears the most secret sins, as well as those which might occasion public disgrace; yea, he fears, lest by a precipitate and inconsiderate conduct he could contract guilt before he is aware. He fears, lest he should inadvertently injure and grieve others, even the weakest and the meanest. He fears using his *liberty*, in a manner that might ensnare his brethren, or might occasion any scandal to a Christian profession: for such is the sensibility of his heart in this respect, that he would be more deeply concerned for the dishonor brought to God, and the reproach which might be thrown on religion by any unsuitable conduct of his, than merely for that part of the shame that might immediately and directly fall upon himself. But again,

5. The regenerate man has *new joys.*

These arise chiefly from an intercourse with God through Jesus Christ; and from a review of himself, as under the sanctifying influences of his grace, and as brought into a state of favor with him, in proportion to the degree in which he can discern himself in this character and state.

You know David, speaking of God, calls him *his exceeding joy;* (Psal. xliii. 4;) and declares *the gladness he had put into his heart,* by *lift-*

ing up the light of his countenance upon him, to be far beyond what *they* could have, *whose corn and wine increased.* Psal. iv. 6, 7. And the Apostle Paul speaks of Christians, as *joying in God through Jesus Christ,* (Rom. v. 11,) and as *rejoicing in Christ Jesus:* (Phil. iii. 3:) and Peter also describes them as those, who, *believing in him, though unseen, rejoice with joy unspeakable, and full of glory.* 1 Pet. i. 8.

Perhaps there was a time, when the good man censured all pretences of this kind, now at least in these latter days of Christianity, as an empty, enthusiastic pretence; but since he has *tasted that the Lord is gracious,* (1 Pet. ii. 3,) he has that experimental knowledge of their reality and excellence, which he can confidently oppose to all the most artful and sophistical cavils; and could as soon doubt, whether the sun enlightens his eyes, and warms his body, as he could question, whether God has ways of manifesting himself to souls, when it is felt with unutterable delight: and when thus entertained, he can adopt David's words, and say, that *his soul is satisfied as with marrow and fatness,* so that *with joyful lips he praises God,* (Psal. lxiii. 5,) when *his meditation of him is* thus *sweet,* (Psal. civ. 34,) and *God says unto his soul, I am thy salvation.* Psal. xxxv. 3.

The survey of the Lord Jesus Christ gives him also unutterable joy; while he reflects on that ample provision, which God has made by him, for the supply of all his necessities; and that firm security which is given to his soul by a believing union with Christ; whereby his life is connected with that of his Saviour. In his constant presence, in his faithful care, he can *boast all the day long;* (Psal. xliv. 8;) and that friendship, which establishes a community of interest between him and his Lord, engages him to rejoice in that salvation and happiness, to which he is advanced *at the right hand of God,* and gives him, by joyful sympathy, his part with Christ in glory, before he personally arrives at the full possession of it. John xiv. 28; Ephes. ii. 6.

I add, that he also rejoices in the consciousness of God's gracious work upon his own soul, so far as he can discern the traces of it there. He delights to feel himself, as it were, cured of the mortal disease with which he once saw himself infected; to find himself in health and vigor of mind, renewed to a conformity with the Divine Image. He delights to look inward, and see that transformation of soul, which has made the *wilderness like the garden of the Lord,* (Isa. li. 3,) so that *instead of the thorn there shall come up the fir-tree, and instead of the brier, the myrtle.* Isa. lv. 13.

Thus the good man is *satisfied from himself:* (Prov. xiv. 14 :) and though he humbly refers the ultimate glory of all to that God, by whose *grace he is what he is,* (1 Cor. xv. 10,) he enters with pleasure into his own mind, and reckons it a part of gratitude to his great Benefactor, to enjoy with as high a relish as he can, the present workings of divine grace within him, as well as the pleasing prospect of what it will farther do.

But this head has so near a resemblance to some that are to follow, that were I to enlarge upon it, as I easily might, I should leave room for nothing different to be said upon them. I will only add,

6. That as the counterpart of this, *new sorrows* will arise in the mind of a regenerate man.

These are particularly such as spring—from the *withdrawings of God's presence*—from the *remains of sin in the soul*—and from the *prevalence of it in the world about him.*

The regenerate man will mourn, when the reviving manifestations of God's presence are withdrawn from his soul. It seems very absurd to interpret the numberless passages in the sacred writers, in which they complain of the *hidings of God's face from them,* as if they merely referred to the want of temporal enjoyments, or to the pressure of temporal calamities. If *the light of*

God's countenance, which they so expressly oppose to temporal blessings, signify a spiritual enjoyment, the want of it must relate to spiritual desertion. And I believe there are few Christians in the world, who are entirely unacquainted with this. They have most of them their seasons, when they *walk in darkness, and see* little or *no light:* (Isa. l. 10:) and this not only when anxious fears arise with relation to their own spiritual state; but at some other times, when, though they can in the main call God *their father*, yet he seems, as it were, *to stand afar off*, and to continue them at a distance, which wears the face of unkindness, especially under temptations and other afflictions, in which they lose their lively sense of God's presence, and that endearing freedom of converse with him, which, through the influence of *the Spirit of adoption* on their souls, they have sometimes known. If this be mysterious and unintelligible to some of you, I am heartily sorry for it; but I do not remember that I was ever intimately acquainted with any one, who seemed to me a real Christian, that has not, upon mentioning the case, acknowledged, that he has felt something of it. At least I will boldly venture to say this, that if you are truly regenerate, and do not know what I mean by it, it is because you have hitherto been kept in a continual flow of holy joy, or at least in a calm and cheerful persuasion of your interest in the Divine favor: and even such may see the day, when *strong* as their *mountain* seems to *stand*, *God may hide his face to their trouble:* (Psal. xxx. 7:) or, however, they will infer from what they now feel, that it must be a mournful case whenever it occurs; and that sorrow, in such circumstance, will soon strike on a truly sanctified heart, and wound it very deep.

The sorrow of a good man also arises "from the remains of sin in his soul." Though he is *upright before God*, and proves it by *keeping himself from his iniquity;* (Psal. xviii. 23;) yet he cries out, *Who can understand his errors?* Psal. xix. 12. *Who can say I have made my heart clean, I am pure from my sin?* Prov. xx. 9. A sense of the sinfulness of his nature humbles him in the dust; and the first risings of irregular inclinations and passions give him a tender pain, with which a carnal heart is unacquainted, even when sin is domineering within him.

And once more, "The prevalence of sin in the world around him," is a grief to one that is born of God. It pierces him to the heart to see men dishonoring God, and ruining themselves: he *beholds transgressors*, as David well expresses it, with a mixture of *indignation* and *sorrow;* (Psal. cxxxix. 21;) and when he seriously considers how common, and yet how sad a case it is, he can perhaps borrow the words of the same prophet, so far as to say, that *rivers of waters run down his eyes, because men keep not the law of God.* Psal. cxix. 136. Now, as these are sorrows that seldom do at all affect the heart of an unregenerate man, I thought it the more proper to mention them, to assist you in your inquiries into your own state.

Such are the affections of love and aversion, of desire and fear, of joy and sorrow, which fill the breast of the regenerate man, and naturally arise from those new apprehensions which are described under the former head. I add,

III. That he has also *new* RESOLUTIONS.

You will easily apprehend I speak of those that are formed for the service of God, and against sin. I readily acknowledge, that there are often, in unregenerate men, some resolutions of this kind, and perhaps those very warm, and for the present very sincere; yet there is considerable difference between them and those we are now to represent; as the resolutions of the truly good man are more *universal*, more *immediate*, and more *humble.*

1. The *resolutions* which he now forms, are more *universal* than they ever were before.

He does not now resolve against this or that

sin, but against all; against sin, as sin; as opposite to the holiness of God, and destructive of the honor and happiness of the rational creation. He does not say with Naaman, concerning this or that more convenient iniquity, *the Lord pardon thy servant in this thing;* (2 Kings v. 18;) nor does he resolve to excuse himself in an indulgence, even of *that sin which does most easily beset him;* (Heb. xii. 1;) but rather, in his general determination against sin, and in those solemn engagements, with which such determinations may be attended, he fixes especially upon those sins which he might before have been most ready to accept.

2. The *resolutions* of the regenerate man are more *immediate.*

It very frequently happens, that while others are under awakening impressions, as they see a necessity for parting with their sins, and engaging in what they may call a religious life, they resolve upon it: but then they think it may be delayed a little longer; perhaps a few years, or at least a few weeks or days; or they, perhaps, refer it to some remarkable period which is approaching, which they flatter themselves they shall make yet more remarkable, as the era of their reformation: but, in the mean time, they will take their farewell of their lusts by a few more indulgences:

and thus they delude themselves, and rivet their chains faster than before. But the good man, with David, *makes haste, and delays not to keep the commandments of God.* Psal. cxix. 60. He is like the prodigal, who, as soon as ever he said, *I will arise and go to my father*, immediately *arose and came to him.* Luke xv. 18, 20. He reckons *the time* he has already spent in the service of sin *may suffice*, (1 Pet. v. 3,) and that indeed it is far more than enough: he wishes he could call back that which is past; but he determines, that he will not take one step further in this unhappy path. He fully purposes, that he will never once more deliberately and presumptuously offend God, in any matter, great or small; if anything can be called small, which is a deliberate and apprehended offence; and he determines, that from this moment he will *yield himself to God, as alive from the dead*, and employ *his members as instruments of righteousness.* Rom. vi. 13. But then,

3. His *resolutions* are more *modest* and *humble* than they have ever been before.

And this indeed is the great circumstance that renders them more effectual. When an awakened sinner feels himself most enslaved to his vices, he pleases himself with this thought, that there is a secret kind of spring in his mind, which, when he pleases to exert, he can break through all at once, and commence, whenever the necessity comes upon him, a very religious man in a moment. And when conscience presses him with the memory of past guilt, and the representation of *future danger*, he cuts off these remonstrances with a hasty resolve, "I will do so no more;" but then, perhaps, the effects of this may not last a day; though possibly it may, at other times, continue a few weeks or months, where the grosser acts of sin are concerned: and indeed his resolutions seldom reach farther than these; for the necessity of a sanctified heart is a mystery which he has never yet learned. But a truly regenerate man has learned wisdom from this experience of his own, and the observation of other men's frailty. He feels his own weakness, and is so thoroughly aware of the treachery of his own heart, that he is almost afraid to express in words the purpose which his very soul is forming: he is almost afraid to turn that purpose into a vow before God, lest the breach of that vow should increase his guilt: but this he can say, with repenting Ephraim, *Lord turn thou me, and I shall be turned;* (Jer. xxxi. 18;) and with David, *Hold up my goings in thy paths, that my footsteps may not slip.* Psal. xvii. 5. "I am exceeding frail; but, Lord, *be thou surety for thy servant for good,* (Psal. cxix. 122,) and then I shall be safe! Do thou rescue me from temptations, and I shall be delivered! Do thou fill my heart with holy sentiments, and I will breathe them out before thee! Do thou excite and maintain a zeal for thy service, and then I will exert myself in it!" And when once a man is come to such a distrust of himself; when, *like a little child,* he stretches out his hand to be led by his heavenly Father, and trusts in his guardian care alone for his security and comfort; then *out of weakness he is made strong,* (Heb. xi. 34,) and goes on safe though trembling; and sees those that made the loudest boasts, and placed the greatest confidence in themselves, *falling on the right hand and on the left,* and their bravery melting away like snow before the sun.

IV. The regenerate man has *new* LABORS and EMPLOYMENTS.

Not that his former employment in secular life is laid aside: it would ordinarily be a very dangerous snare for a man to imagine that God requires this. On the contrary, the Apostle gives it in charge to Christian converts, that *in what calling soever a man is found when he is called* into the profession of the Gospel, *he should therein abide with God.* 1 Cor. vii. 20, 24. But when he becomes a real Christian he prosecutes this calling, whatever it be, with a new spirit and temper, from new principles, and to new purposes.

While his hands are laboring in the world, his heart is often rising to God; he consecrates his work to the Divine honor, and to the credit of religion; and desires, that *his merchandise* and his gain *may*, in this sense, *be holiness to the Lord*, (Isa. xxiii. 18,) by employing it to support the family which Providence has committed to his charge, (1 Tim. v. 8,) and to relieve the poor whom Christ recommends to his pity; (Acts xx. 35;) and as he depends upon God to give him wisdom and success in the conduct of his affairs, he ascribes the glory of that success to him; not *sacrificing to his own net, nor burning incense to his own drag.* Hab. i. 16.

And I will further add, that regeneration introduces a set of new labors, added to the former, with which the man was before utterly unacquainted. We may consider, as the principal and chief of these, the great labor of purifying the heart, of conquering sinful inclinations, and affections, and of approaching God by a more intimate access and more endeared converse. Now they that imagine this to be an easy matter, know little of the human heart, little of the spirituality of God's nature, and his law.

Give me leave to say, that the labors of the body, in cultivating the earth, are much more easily performed than this spiritual husbandry. To weed a soil so luxuriant in evil productions, and to raise a plentiful harvest of holy affections and actions in a soil so barren of good; to regulate appetites and passions so exorbitant as those of the human heart naturally are, and to awaken in it suitable affections; to be abundant in the fruits of righteousness, and to converse with God in the exercise of devotion: these are no little things; nor will a little resolution, watchfulness, and activity suffice, in order to the discharge of such a business. It is comparatively easy to go through the forms of prayer and praise, whatever they are: to read, or from present conception to utter, a few words before God: but to unite the heart in God's service, to wrestle with him for a blessing, to pour out the heart before him, to speak to him as searching the very heart; so that He should say, "This is prayer:" this, my brethren, is a work indeed; and he that is conscientious in the discharge of it will find, that it is not to be dispatched in a few hasty moments, nor without serious reflection, and a resolute watch maintained over the spirit.

New labors also arise to the regenerate soul, in consequence of the concern it has to promote religion in the world. Being possessed, as I formerly showed you the heart of the good man is, with an unfeigned love to his fellow-creatures, and knowing of how great importance religion is to the happiness of men, he pleads earnestly with God for the propagation and success of the Gospel: and he endeavors, according to his ability and opportunity, to promote it; to promote *pure and undefiled religion* in his family and his neighborhood, even in all around him. And this requires observation and application, that this attempt may be prudently conducted, and great resolution, in order to its being rendered effectual: it requires great diligence in watching over ourselves, lest our examples prove inconsistent with our precepts; and no small degree of courage, considering how averse the generality of mankind are to admonitions and reproofs; in consequence of which, a person can hardly act the part of a faithful friend, without exposing himself to the hazard of being accounted an enemy.

Such are the new labors of the real Christian. Let any man try to perform them, and he will not find them light; but to encourage the attempt, let me further add,

V. That the regenerate soul has its *new* ENTERTAINMENTS too.

He has *pleasures*, which *a stranger intermeddles not with*, (Prov. xiv. 10,) and which *the world* can neither *give*, nor *take away:* (John xvi. 22:)

pleasures, which a thousand times overbalance the most painful labors, and the most painful sufferings too; and which, sweetly mingling themselves with the various circumstances of life, through which the Christian passes, do, as it were, gild all the scene, and make all the fatigues and self-denial of his life far more agreeable, than any of those delights the worldling, or the sensualist, can find in the midst of his unbounded and studied indulgences. But here I shall be in great danger of repeating what I said under a former head, when I was speaking of the new joys which the Christian feels, in consequence of the great change that regeneration makes in his soul: and therefore, omitting what I then observed, concerning the pleasure of communion with God through Christ, and of perceiving a work of Divine grace upon the soul, I shall now touch upon some other sources of exalted entertainment, which did not so directly fall under that head.

1. The Christian finds *new pleasures* in the *word of God.*

You know with what relish the saints of old spake of it. *Thy words were found*, says the Prophet, *and I did eat them; and thy word was unto me the joy and rejoicing of mine heart.* Jer. xv. 16. *Thy statutes*, says the Psalmist, *are more to be desired than gold, yea, than much fine gold:*

they are sweeter also than honey, and the honey-comb. Psal. xix. 10. The apostle Peter beautifully represents this, when he exhorts the saints to whom he wrote, *as new-born babes to desire the sincere milk of the word, that they might grow thereby.* 1 Pet. ii. 2. And the infant that smiles on the breast, and with such eagerness and delight draws its nourishment from it, seems an amiable image of the humble Christian, who *receives the kingdom of God*, and the word of that kingdom, *as a little child;* (Mark x. 15;) who *lays up* Scripture *in his heart*, (Job xxii. 22,) and draws forth the sweetness of it, with a firm persuasion, that it is indeed the word of God, and was appointed by him for the food of his soul.

2. He also finds *new pleasures* in the *ordinances of Divine worship.*

He is *glad when it is said unto him, Let us go into the house of the Lord.* Psal. cxxii. 1 He indeed esteems the *tabernacles of the Lord*, as *amiable*, and regards *a day in his courts as better than a thousand* elsewhere. Psal. lxxxiv. 1, 10. And this pleasure arises, not merely from anything peculiar in the administrations of this or that man who officiates in holy things; but from the nature of the exercise in general, and from a regard to the Divine authority of those institutions which are there observed. He feels a sacred delight in an intercourse with God in those solemnities; in comparison of which, all the graces of composition and delivery appear as little as the harmony of instruments, or the perfume of incense, to one of the Old Testament saints, when compared with *the light of God's countenance*, which was *lifted up* on the pious worshipers under the Mosaic forms, *when in his temple every one spake of his glory.* Psal. xxix. 9. *One thing has he desired of the Lord*, and *that he seeks after, that he may dwell in the house of the Lord all the days of his life;* not to amuse his vain imagination, not to gratify his ear, not to indulge his curiosity with useless inquiries, nor merely to exercise his understanding with sublime speculations; but *to behold the beauty of the Lord, and to inquire in his temple.* Psal. xxxvii. 4.

3. He likewise finds a *new entertainment* in the *conversation of Christian friends.*

He now knows what it is to have *fellowship with those* whose *communion is with the Father, and with his Son Jesus Christ.* 1 John i. 3. His *delight is* now *in them* that are truly *the excellent of the earth.* Psal. xvi. 3. He delights to dismiss the usual topics of modern conversation, that some religious subject may be taken up, not as matter of dispute, but as matter of devout recollection; and loves to hear the plainest Christian express his experimental sense of divine things. Those sentiments of piety and love, which come warm from a gracious heart, are always pleasing to him; and those appear the dearest bands of friendship, which may draw him nearer to his heavenly Father, and unite his soul in ties of more ardent love to his Redeemer. A society of such friends is indeed a kind of anticipation of heaven; and to choose, and to delight in such, is no contemptible token, that the soul has attained to some considerable degree of preparation for it. I only add,

VI. That in consequence of all this, the regenerate soul has *new* HOPES and PROSPECTS.

Men might be very much assisted in judging of their true state, if they would seriously reflect what it is they hope and wish for. What are those expectations and desires that most strongly impress their minds? A vain mortal, untaught and unchanged by Divine grace, is always dressing up to himself some empty phantom of earthly happiness, which he looks after and pursues, and foolishly imagines, "Could I grasp it, and keep it, I should be happy." But Divine grace teaches the real Christian to give up these empty schemes. "God," he says, "never intended this world for my happiness: he will make it tolerable to me; he will give me so much of it as he sees consistent with my highest interest; he will enable me to derive instruction, and it may be consolation, out of its disappointments and distresses: but he reserves my inheritance for the eternal world. I am *begotten again to a lively hope, by the resurrection of Jesus Christ from the dead,* even *to* the hope of *an inheritance incorruptible, and undefiled, and that fadeth not away;* (1 Pet. i. 3, 4:) and though it be, for the present *reserved in heaven,* it is so safe, and so great, that it is well worth my waiting for, though ever so long; *for the things that are not seen, are eternal.*" 2 Cor. iv. 18.

And this indeed is the true character of a good man. Eternity fills his thoughts; and growing sensible, in another manner than he ever was before, of the importance of it, he pants after the enjoyment of eternal happiness. Assign any limited duration to his enjoyment of God in the regions of glory, and you would overwhelm him with disappointment: talk of hundreds, of thousands, of millions of years, the disappointment is almost equal: periods like these seem scarce distinguishable from each other, when compared with an eternal hope. To eternity his desires and expectations are raised; and he can be contented with nothing less than eternity; perfect holiness, and perfect happiness for ever and ever, without any mixture of sin, or any alloy of sorrow; this he firmly expects, this he ardently breathes after; a felicity which an immortal soul shall never outlive, and which an eternal God shall never cease to communicate. This heavenly country he seeks; he considers himself as a citizen of it, and endeavors to maintain *his conversation* there; (Phil. iii. 20;) to carry on, as it were, a daily trade for heaven, and to *lay up a treasure there;* (Matt. vi. 20;) in which he may be rich and great, when all the pomp of this earth is passed away as a dream, and all its most precious metals and gems are melted down and consumed among its vilest materials in the last universal burning.

This is the change, the glorious change, which regeneration makes in a man's character and views; and who shall dare to speak, or to think contemptibly of it? Were we indeed to represent it as a kind of charm, depending on an external ceremony, which it was the peculiar prerogative of a certain order of men to perform, and yet on which eternal life was suspended; one might easily apprehend, that it would be brought into much suspicion. Or should we place it in any mechanical transports of animal nature, in any blind impulse, in any strong feelings, not to be described, or accounted for, or argued upon, but known by some inward inexplicable sensation to be divine; we could not wonder, if calm and prudent men were slow to admit the pretension to it, and were fearful it might end in the most dangerous enthusiasm, made impious by excessive appearances of piety. But when it is delineated by such fair and bright characters as those that have now been drawn; when these divine lineaments on the soul, by which it bears the image of its Maker's rectitude and sanctity, are considered as its necessary consequence, or rather as its very essence; one would imagine, that every rational creature, instead of caviling at it, should pay an immediate homage to it, and earnestly desire, and labor, and pray, to experience the change: especially as it is a change so desirable for itself—as we acknowledge health to be, though a man were not to be rewarded for doing well, nor punished, any farther than with the malady he contracts, for any negligence in this respect.

Where is there anything can be more ornamental to our natures, than to have all the powers of the mind thus changed by grace, and our pursuits directed to such objects as are worthy of the best attention and regard?—to have our apprehensions of divine and spiritual things enlarged, and to have right conceptions of the most important matters;—to have the stream of our affections turned from empty vanities, to objects that are proper to excite and fix them;—to have our resolutions set against all sin, and a full purpose formed within us of an immediate reformation and return to God, with a dependence on his grace to help us *both to will and to do;*—to have our labors steadfastly applied to conquer sin, and to promote religion in ourselves and others; to have our entertainments founded in a religious life, and flowing in upon us from the sweet intercourse we have with God in his word and ordinances, and the delightful conversation that we sometimes have with Christian friends;—and finally, to have our hopes drawn off from earthly things, and fixed upon eternity?

Where is there anything can be more honorable to us, than thus to be *renewed after the image of him that created us*, (Col. iii. 10,) and to *put on the new man, which after God is created in righteousness and true holiness?* Eph. iv. 24. And where is anything that can be more desirable, than thus to have the darkness of our understandings cured, and the disorders rectified, that sin had brought upon our nature? Who is there that is so insensible of his depravity, as that he would not long for such a happy change? Or who is there that knows how excellent a work it is, to be *transformed by the renewing of the mind*, (Rom. xii. 2,) that would not, with the greatest thankfulness, adore the riches of Divine grace, if it appear that he is thus become *a new creature;* that *old things are passed away, and behold, all things are become new?*

But I shall quickly show you, that regeneration is not only ornamental, honorable, and desirable, but absolutely necessary, as ever we would hope to share the blessings of God's heavenly kingdom, and to escape the horror of those that are finally and irrevocably excluded from it. This argument will employ several succeeding Discourses.

But I would dismiss you at present with an earnest request, that you would, in the mean time, renew your inquiries, as to the truth of regeneration in your own souls; which, after all that I have been saying, it will be very inexcusable for you to neglect, as probably you will hear few discourses, in the whole course of your lives, which centre more directly in this point, or are more industriously calculated to give you the safest and clearest assistance in it. May God abase the arrogance and presumption of every self-deceiving sinner; and awaken the confidence and joy of the feeblest soul, in whom this new creation is begun!

DISCOURSE IV.

THE NECESSITY OF REGENERATION, ARGUED FROM THE IMMUTABLE CONSTITUTION OF GOD.

JOHN III. 3.

Jesus answered and said unto him, Verily, verily, I say unto thee, Except a man be born again, he cannot see the kingdom of God.

WHILE the ministers of Christ are discoursing of such a subject, as I have before me in the course of these Lectures, and particularly in this branch of them which I am now entering upon, we may surely, with the utmost reason, address our hearers in those words of Moses to Israel, in the conclusion of his dying discourse: *Set your hearts unto all the words which I testify among you this day, which ye shall command your children to observe and do,* even *all the words of this law; for it is not a vain thing for you, because it is your life.* Deut. xxxii. 46, 47. That must undoubtedly be your life, concerning which the Lord Jesus Christ himself, the incarnate wisdom of God, *the faithful and true witness,* (Rev. iii. 14,) has said, and said it with a solemn repeated asseveration, that without it *a man cannot see the kingdom of God.*

The occasion of his saying it deserves our notice; though the niceties of the context must be waived in such a series of sermons as this. He said it to a Jew of considerable rank, and, as it appears, one of the grand Sanhedrim, or chief council of the nation; who came not only for his own private satisfaction, but in the name of several of his brethren, to discourse with Christ concerning his doctrine, at the first passover he attended at Jerusalem, after he had entered on his public ministry. Our Lord would, to be sure, be peculiary careful what answer he returned to such an inquiry: and this is his answer, *Verily, verily, I say unto thee, Except a man be born again, he cannot see the kingdom of God:* as if he should have said, "If the princes of Israel inquire after my character, let them know that I came to be a preacher of *regeneration;* and that the blessings of that kingdom, which I am come to reveal and erect, are to be peculiar to renewed and sanctified souls; who may, by an easy and natural figure, be said *to be born again.*" And the figure appears very intelligible, and very instructive to those that will seriously consider it; and might well lead us into a variety of pertinent and useful remarks.

You easily perceive, that to be born again must intimate a very great change; coming, as it were, into a new world, as an infant does; when after having lived awhile a kind of vegetative life in the darkness and confinement of the womb, it is born into open day; feels the vital air rushing in on its lungs, and light forcing itself upon the awakened eyes; hears sounds before unknown; opens its mouth to receive a yet untasted food, and every day becomes acquainted with new objects, and exerts new powers, till it grows up to the maturity of a perfect man. Such, and in some respects greater and nobler than this, is the change which regeneration makes in a heart, before unacquainted with religion: as you may have seen at large from the preceding discourses.

But I might further observe, that the phrase in the text may also express the humbling nature of this change, as well as the greatness of it. Erasmus gives this turn to the words; and it is so edifying, that I should have mentioned it at least, though I had not thought it so just, as it appears. *To be born again*, must signify *to become as a little child;* (Matt. xviii. 3;) and our Lord expressly and frequently assures us, that without this *we cannot enter into the kingdom of heaven.*

Mark x. 15; Luke xviii. 17. He has pronounced the very first of his blessings on *poverty of spirit;* (Matt. v. 3;) and where this is wanting, the soul will never be entitled to the rest. A mild and humble, a docile and tractable temper, a freedom from avarice and ambition, and an indifference to those great toys of which men are generally so fond, are all essential parts of the Christian character; and they have all, in one view or another, been touched upon in the preceding discourses. Let it be forgiven, however, if considering the importance of the case, you are told again, that *in malice ye must be children;* (1 Cor. xiv. 20;) and that *if any man think himself wise, he must become* a child, and even a *fool, that he may be wise* indeed. 1 Cor. iii. 18.

I might observe once more, that these words intimate the divine power, by which this great and humbling change is effected. Our first formation and birth is the work of God, and no less really so in the succeeding generations of men, than the first production of Adam was, when *God formed him of the dust of the earth, and breathed into his nostrils the breath of life.* Gen. ii. 7. We may each of us say, with respect to the natural birth, and in an accommodated sense with respect to the spiritual too, *thine eyes did see my substance, being as yet imperfect, and in thy book all my members, which in continuance* of time *were fashioned, were written, when as yet there was none of them.* Psal. cxxxix. 16. All the first gracious impressions that were made upon the mind, and all the gradual advances of them, till Christ was formed in the heart, and the new creature animated, must, as I shall hereafter show at large, be ultimately and principally referred into a divine operation; and in this sense, it is God that brings every good purpose in the mind to the birth, and God that *gives strength to bring forth.* Isa. lxvi. 9.

But I omit the farther prosecution of these remarks at present, because they coincide with what I have said in former discourses, or what will occur in those which are yet to come: and shall only further consider the words, as they are a confirmation of, and therefore a proper introduction to, what I am to lay before you under the third general head of these discourses; in which—as I have already shown who may be said to be in an unregenerate state, and how great that change is which regeneration makes in the soul—I shall now proceed,

Thirdly, to show the high importance, yea, the absolute NECESSITY of this change.

Our Lord expresses it in a very lively and awakening manner, in these few determinate words, which are here before us: *Verily, verily, I say unto thee, except a man be born again, he cannot see the kingdom of God.* You see how emphatical the words are: he who is himself invariable truth, *the same yesterday, to-day, and forever,* (Heb. xiii. 8,) repeats it again and again, with as much solemnity as he ever uses upon any occasion; repeats it to us, as he did to Nicodemus, "*Verily, verily, I say unto you,* that is, I seriously deliver it as a truth of infinite moment; *except a man,* i. e. any man, whatever his profession, whatever his knowledge, or whatever his privileges, may be; though he be a Jew, though he be a Pharisee, though he be, as thou Nicodemus art, a ruler or a senator; except he *be born again,* and have that great change, so often described in the word of God, wrought by the operation of the Spirit in his mind, *he cannot see the kingdom of God:* he cannot by any means approach it so as to enter into it, or have any share in the important blessings which it contains."

That we may more fully understand, and enter into this weighty argument, I shall from these words,

I. Briefly consider, what it is to *see the kingdom of God.*

II. Show how absolutely impossible it is, that any unregenerate man should *see* it. And,

III. How wretched a thing it is to be deprived of the sight and enjoyment of it.

And I am well persuaded, that if you diligently attend to these things, you will be inwardly and powerfully convinced, that no argument could be more proper to demonstrate the *importance* and *necessity* of *regeneration*, than this, which our Lord has suggested in these awful, emphatical, and comprehensive words.

I. I am to show you what it is to *see the kingdom of God.*

And for the explication of it, it will be necessary to consider—what we are to understand by *this kingdom;* and what is meant by *seeing it.*

I will show you now what we are to understand by *the kingdom of God.* And you will pardon me if I state the matter pretty largely; because the phrase is used in scripture in different senses; and the true interpretation of many passages in it depends on a proper distinction between them. You may observe then, for the explication of this phrase, that the kingdom of God in general signifies, 'the society of those, who profess themselves the servants and subjects of Christ;' and in consequence of this, that there are some passages, in which it peculiarly relates to the imperfect dispensation of this kingdom, and the beginning of it in the world; and others, in which it relates to the more perfect form, which this society is to bear in the world of glory.

1. The *kingdom of God*, or the *kingdom of heaven*—for they are synonymous phrases—does in the general signify *the society of those, who profess themselves the servants and subjects of Christ.*

You well know this was a phrase used among the Jews: and therefore the original of it is to be traced from the Old Testament; and I apprehend it to be this: Almost every Christian is aware, that in the early days of the Jewish commonwealth, as Samuel with great propriety expresses it, *God was their king.* 1 Sam. xii. 12. Jehovah was not only the great object of their religious regard, as the creator and supporter of the whole world; but he was also their supreme civil magistrate, settling the forms of their political government, and reserving to himself some of the chief acts of royal authority. They did indeed afterwards *desire another king, like the other nations* around about them. 1 Sam. viii. 5. But still those kings, being appointed by God, were indeed to be looked upon as no other than his vicegerents, though another kind of governors than he had originally instituted.

By degrees their peculiar regard to the civil authority of God among them, as well as to his religious authority, which was nearly connected with it, in a great measure wore out; and their government went through a great many different forms, which it would be unnecessary here particularly to describe. Nevertheless, God was pleased to declare by king David, and by many others of his holy prophets, that he would in due time interpose to erect another, and a far more extensive kingdom in the world; not indeed upon the same political principles with that which he exercised over the Jews; which principles would by no means have suited this extensive design: but it should be a kingdom in which the authority of the *God of heaven* should be acknowledged, and his laws of universal righteousness observed with greater care, and to nobler purposes, as well as by a vastly greater number of subjects than ever before. *This kingdom* he determined to commit to the government of the Messiah, who, with regard to this was called *the Lord's anointed, his king whom he set upon his holy hill of Zion;* (Psal. ii. 2, 6;) and to whom indeed he would *give all power*, not only *on earth*, but *in heaven* too; (Matt. xxviii. 18;) so that having trained up his subjects here, in the discipline of holiness and obedience, he should at length translate them to another and a *better country, that is, a heavenly,* where they should *see his glory*, and should *reign with him* in eternal life

This plainly appears from the whole tenor of the Old and New Testament, to have been the grand plan of God, with respect to the Messiah's kingdom: and you will easily see, that coming from God as its great author, and referring to him as its end, it may, with great propriety, be called the *kingdom of God;* and ultimately terminating in the heavenly state, it may also properly be called the *kingdom of heaven.* These were phrases, which prevailed in the Jewish nation, before Christ, or his immediate forerunner appeared; and indeed they were used by Daniel in a very remarkable manner, which probably made them so familiar to the Jews, who had some peculiar reason for studying his writings, even more than those of some other prophets. After that prophet had foretold the rise and fall of several great empires of the world, he adds, *and in the days of these* last *kings,* i. e. of the Romans, *shall the God of Heaven set up a kingdom which shall not be destroyed,—but shall stand forever.* Dan. ii. 44. And the person whom *the Ancient of Days,* i. e. the eternal and ever blessed God, should fix on the throne of *this kingdom,* from his appearing in the human nature, is called *the Son of Man;* (Dan. vii. 13, 14;) "I saw in the night visions, and behold, one like the Son of Man, came with the clouds of heaven, and came to the Ancient of

Days, and they brought him near before him; and there was given him dominion, and glory, and a kingdom, that all people, nations, and languages, should serve him: his dominion is an everlasting dominion, which shall not pass away, and his kingdom that which shall not be destroyed."

In allusion to this, when our Lord Jesus Christ appeared, he called himself *the Son of Man;* and he particularly used this phrase, and it was exceedingly proper that he should, in this conference with Nicodemus, again and again. John iii. 13, 14. And all those who, being convinced of the divine commission he bore, submitted themselves to him, might in this respect be said, *to enter into the kingdom of God*, or *of heaven:* that is, into the society which had so long been foretold and expected under that title. *This kingdom*, as the above mentioned prophecy declared, was to be raised from very low beginnings, and under the personal ministry of Christ and his Apostles, till at last it should extend through very distant regions of the world, and kings and princes should submit themselves to it, and reckon it their glory to enroll themselves among his subjects.

Agreeably to this meaning of the phrase, and to this view with respect to the establishment of *his kingdom*, our Lord opened his ministry with preaching, as John the Baptist had done, *the kingdom of heaven.* Matt. iii. 2; iv. 17. And you will see, that in most places of the Gospel, where the phrase occurs, it is to be taken in this sense. Thus our Lord says, *Blessed are the poor in spirit; for theirs is the kingdom of heaven;* (Matt. v. 3;) i. e. they are fit to be members of this society, and to receive the blessings of it. *Seek first the kingdom of God, and his righteousness;* (Matt. vi. 33;) i. e. labor to serve the interests of this society that I am erecting, and to obtain and promote that righteousness which it recommends, and is intended to establish in the world. And again, *Suffer little children to come unto me, and forbid them not; for of such is the kingdom of God:* (Luke xviii. 16;) persons with such a disposition are most fit to become my subjects, and to enter into this holy and spiritual society. And when our Lord says to the Pharisees, *Publicans and harlots go into the kingdom of God before you;* (Mark xxi. 31;) he means, no doubt, they are more ready than you to join themselves to the society of those who profess themselves my subjects. And once more, when he speaks of some who chose the severities of a single life, that with less entanglements they might serve the interests of his church, he expresses it, by their *making themselves eunuchs, for the kingdom of heaven's sake.* Matt. xiv. 12.

I shall only add, that the phrase, by a near connection with this sense, sometimes signifies the *character* of this society, or the privileges which it affords to its members; as when our Lord says, *Whosoever shall not receive the kingdom of God as a little child, shall in no wise enter therein.* Luke xviii. 17.

This then is the general sense of this phrase; it signifies the society of those who should submit themselves to the government of Christ, as appointed by God to rule over them; who are thereby to be considered as God's people and subjects. In consequence of this you will easily apprehend,

2. That it comprehends *the more imperfect dispensation,* under which the members of this society are, during their abode *in the present world.*

All that passes here is indeed but the opening of Christ's kingdom: nevertheless, the phrase does sometimes more particularly refer to this opening; and there are several passages, in which it would be apparently absurd to suppose it comprehended the glories of the invisible state, to which Christ intended finally to conduct his faithful servants. Thus our Lord tells the Pharisees, *The kingdom of God is come unto you,* (Matt. xii.

28,) i. e. that gracious dispensation under the Messiah, by which God is gathering subjects to his Son. And elsewhere he says to them, *The kingdom of God cometh not with observation*, i. e. not with such outward show and grandeur as you expect; but *behold it is within*, or, (as it might be rendered,) *among you;* (Luke xvii. 20, 21;) God has begun to open and establish it, though you know it not; and has actually brought many poor sinners into it, whom you proudly deride as ignorant and accursed. Thus also, when our Lord says to Peter, *I will give unto thee the keys of the kingdom of heaven*, (Matt. xvi. 19,) it would be most absurd to suppose, he meant to grant to him the power of admitting into, or excluding from, the world of glory: but the plain meaning is, that he should bear office in the church on earth, and be the means of admitting Jews and Gentiles into it. Here, as in many other instances, the *kingdom of God*, or *of heaven*, means much the same with the professing church of Christ, in this imperfect state; as it undoubtedly does, when Christ threatens his hearers, that *the kingdom of God should be taken away from them;* (Matt. xxi. 43;) and when he represents it as consisting of *good* and *bad*, (Matt. xiii. 48,) of *tares* and *wheat;* (Verse 25,) but declares, that at the last day he will *gather out of his kingdom all things that of-*

fend, and them that do iniquity; (Matt. xiii. 41;) whereas nothing of that kind shall ever enter into the kingdom of glory. But yet,

3. It ultimately relates to *the more perfect form* and state of this society *in the kingdom of glory.*

You very well know, that the design of God in his Gospel was not to establish a temporal kingdom, as the Jews expected: nor merely to form a body of men, who should live upon earth with some peculiar forms of worship, under very excellent rules, and with distinguished privileges of a spiritual nature; but that all these ultimately referred to the invisible world. Thither *the Son of Man* was removed, when he had finished the scenes of his labor and sufferings upon earth; and thither all the true and faithful members of the kingdom were sooner or later to be brought, and there were to have their final settlement and everlasting abode, in a far more splendid and happy state, than the greatest monarch on earth has ever known: they shall there, as the Apostle most properly expresses it, *reign in life by Jesus Christ.* Rom. v. 17.

Now as the kingdom of God upon earth is to be considered with a leading view to this, so we sometimes find, that this glorious state of its members, or which will come much to the same thing, the society of the faithful in this glorious state, is, by way of eminence, called *the kingdom of God:* and with regard to this, they whose characters are such that they shall be excluded from thence, are represented as having *no part in the kingdom of heaven,* though they have been by profession members of the church of Christ on earth. Of this you have a remarkable instance, where our Lord says, *Not every one that saith unto me, Lord, Lord, shall enter into the kingdom of heaven: but he that doth the will of my Father which is in heaven:* (Matt. vii. 21:) now it was calling Christ, Lord, or professing a regard to him as a divine teacher and governor, which was the very circumstance that distinguished the members of his kingdom on earth from the rest of mankind: yet as they who do this insincerely shall be excluded from final glory, it is said, *they shall not enter into the kingdom of heaven.* So also the Apostle tells us, that *flesh and blood,* i. e. such gross machines of animal nature as those in which we now dwell, *cannot inherit the kingdom of God;* (2 Cor. xv. 50;) they cannot dwell in so pure a region; and therefore it is necessary, that before they enter upon it, those who are found alive at the illustrious day of Christ's appearance, should undergo a miraculous change to fit them for such an abode. In reference to this we are likewise told, that *then,* i. e. at the great resurrection-day, *the righteous shall shine forth as the sun in the kingdom of their Father.* Matt. xiii. 43. And this is what our Lord most certainly had in view, when he tells the impenitent Jews, that *there should be weeping and gnashing of teeth, when they should see Abraham, and Isaac, and Jacob, and all the prophets in the kingdom of God, and they themselves thrust out;* (Luke xiii. 29;) which could not be meant of the privileges of the Christian church upon earth, in which the patriarchs had no share; nor did the Jews at all envy those professing Christians, who most evidently had: it must undoubtedly therefore be numbered among those passages, in which *the kingdom of God* chiefly refers to the state of glory. And I apprehend, the text here before us may be added to that catalogue which leads us to show,

2. What we are to understand by *seeing the kingdom of God.*

Now, in general, you will easily apprehend, that to see the kingdom is to enjoy the blessings of it. There is no need of enumerating many passages of Scripture, where *to see* properly signifies *to enjoy.* This is apparently the sense of it, when Christ declares, *Blessed are the pure in heart; for they shall see God:* (Matt. v. 8:) for the Deity cannot be the object of sight; but the promise is, that such souls—Oh, that we may be in their number!—shall forever enjoy the most delightful communications from him. And thus again we are to understand it, where it is said, *What man is he that desireth life, and loveth many days, that he may see*, i. e. that he may *enjoy*, *good?* Psal. xxxiv. 12. For otherwise, to see it without enjoying it, would be a great aggravation of misery and distress. And in this sense it is most evident, that *seeing the kingdom of God* must here be put, for enjoying the most important blessings appropriated to this state; because, as I have just been observing, condemned sinners are represented in another sense, as seeing that kingdom and the glorified saints in it; but viewing it only at an unapproachable distance, as a spectacle that fills them with horror and despair.

This therefore is, upon the whole, the meaning of this passage: That no unregenerate soul shall finally have any part in the glory and happiness which Christ has prepared for his faithful subjects; nor can any that appear to be such, according to the tenor and constitution of the gospel, be admitted into the number even of professing Christians. It is true, indeed, a man may appear under such a disguise, that those who are in this sense *the stewards of the mysteries of God*, (1 Cor. iv. 1,) may, in the judgment of charity, be obliged to think well of him, and to admit him; but Christ, who intimately knows him, does even now discern him. The present external privileges he enjoys, are such as he has no just right to; and in a little time, Christ will root him out of this kingdom with a vengeance, and he shall be openly declared a rebel, and one whom the *Lord* of it *never knew*, or never approved. Matt. vii. 23. So that upon the whole, it is so little a part that he had in the kingdom, and that for so short a time, that it may, in the free language of Scripture, be said, that he has *never seen the kingdom of God* at all; that he *has neither part nor lot in this matter*, (Acts viii. 21,) has *no part* with God's chosen, *nor any lot* with his inheritance.

Having thus largely explained the meaning of this phrase, I now proceed,

II. To show you how CERTAIN this declaration of our Lord in the text is, or how absolutely impossible it is, that any unregenerate man should thus *see the kingdom of God.*

Now this I shall argue, partly from the *immutable constitution of God*, whose kingdom it is: and partly from the *nature of its blessings*, which are such, that no unregenerate man, while he continues in that state, can have any fitness or capacity to enjoy them.

The first of these considerations is copious and

important enough, to furnish out abundant matter for the remainder of this discourse: and it will be difficult to dispatch it within these limits.

1. The impossibility there is, that any unregenerate man should *enter into the kingdom of God,* appears from the IMMUTABLE CONSTITUTION of that God, whose kingdom it is.

This might be sufficiently argued, from the express and emphatical words of our Lord Jesus Christ in the text. For he bore his Father's commission to preach the *Gospel of the kingdom,* to publish the *good news* of its erection and success, and likewise to declare its nature, and the method of admittance into it. And he is himself the great Sovereign of that kingdom; and consequently cannot but perfectly, and beyond all comparison with any other, know the whole of its constitution. But God has repeated the declaration by him, and by his other messengers to the children of men, in different ages, and under different dispensations, in such a manner as suited its infinite importance. And, therefore, for the further illustration of the argument, I shall enumerate a great variety of scriptures that speak the same language; not so much aiming therein at the speulative proof of the point, as attempting to impress the conscience of my hearers with a sense of its certainty; and humbly hoping that some of those sharp-pointed arrows, which I am now drawing out of the quiver of God, may, by the direction of his Spirit, *enter the reins* of some against whom they are leveled, (Lam. iii. 8,) and convince them of the absolute necessity of an entire change in their hearts, as well as their lives, or of the vanity of all those hopes which they entertain, while that change is wanting. And let me bespeak your attention, not to the conjectures or reasoning of a frail mortal man, but to the solemn admonitions and declarations of the eternal God; and be assured that in one sense or another, *his word shall take hold on you*, as it has done on sinners of former generations, either for conviction, or condemnation.

That I may not be confounded in the multiplicity of my proofs, I shall range them under these three distinct heads. The *prophets* of the Old Testament were commissioned to make this declaration:—it was renewed by the preaching of *Christ*;—and was supported by the testimony of the *Apostles* under the inspiration of the Holy Spirit.

The *prophets* of the Old Testament were commissioned in effect to make this declaration, that no unregenerate sinner should *enter the kingdom of God.*

Well might our Lord say to Nicodemus, *Art thou*

a teacher in Israel, and knowest not these things? For *to this* in effect *all the prophets bear witness,* and it might be learned from almost every page of their writings. It is true the particular phrase of being *born again, or regenerated,* does not occur there; nor is it expressly said, that an unregenerate man shall not be admitted into God's kingdom. But then the prophets everywhere assert, what is in effect the same, that no wicked man, who does not heartily repent of his sins, and turn from them to God, must expect the Divine favor. Now if you consider what we mean by an unregenerate man, according to the description I have given before, you will find it is just the same as an impenitent sinner; and if it be declared that such are not to expect the Divine favor, nay, that they must certainly prove the object of his displeasure, this must certainly imply an exclusion from his kingdom, and must intend a great deal more than being deprived of everlasting happiness. And thus you see that all those scriptures, which speak of the irreconcilable hatred of God against sin, and against all impenitent sinners, come in to do service here, and are equivalent to the declaration in the text. And I may hereafter show you, that there are many scriptures in the Old Testament which lead men to consider that change, said to be so necessary, as what must be effected by a Divine operation on their souls. But as that will more properly come in under a following head, I shall at present content myself with selecting a few scriptures as a specimen of many hundred more, in proof of the main point before us: and I beseech you that you would endeavor to enter, not only into the *sense*, but into the *spirit* of them.

You well know that unregenerate sinners are wicked men; and of such it is said, *God is angry with the wicked every day;* (Psal. vii. 2;) or *all the day long*, as the original imports. The sinner lies down and rises up, goes out and comes in, under the Divine displeasure: and though with great patience God bears with him for awhile, he is described as preparing his dreadful artillery against him, to smite him even with a mortal wound: so far will he be from admitting him into his kingdom, that, as it is there added, if he turn not he will whet his sword; he has bent his bow and made it ready; he has also prepared for him the instruments of death. Psal. vii. 12, 13. And in another place, he describes the dreadful consequence of that preparation in most lively terms: "If I whet my glittering sword, and my hand take hold on judgment, I will render vengeance to mine enemies, and will reward them that hate me: I will make mine arrows drunk with blood, and my sword shall devour flesh, from the beginning of revenges on the enemy;" i. e. as soon as I begin this awful work. Deut. xxxii. 41, 42. And elsewhere he compares the destruction which he will bring upon sinners at last, to that which he executed on Sodom and Gomorrah, when he scattered fire and brimstone on their habitations, and reduced their pleasant country to a burning lake; *Upon the wicked he will rain snares, fire and brimstone, and an horrible tempest; this will be the portion of their cup:* (Psal. xi. 6:) and oh, how unlike the state and abode of those who are the happy subjects of his kingdom!

None of the prophets speak in milder and more gentle language to returning penitents than Isaiah; yet he declares, *there is no peace, saith my God, to the wicked.* Isa. lvii. 21. Yea, he does, as it were, call in the concurrence of all who feared God, and who loved their country, to echo back and enforce the admonition: *say ye to the righteous, that it shall be well with him:* but on the other hand, *wo to the wicked! it shall be ill with him; for the reward of his hands shall be given him.* Isa. iii. 10, 11.

The enumeration would be endless; and it would require more than the time of a whole discourse, only to read over, without any comment or remark one half of the passages which might properly be introduced on this occasion. I will therefore only mention two more, which, though some of you may *hear* with indifference, I confess I cannot *read* without a very sensible inward commotion.

The one is that passage in the Mosaic law, where God directs his servant to say, " If there be among you a root that beareth gall and wormwood, (i. e. any unregenerate soul,) who when he hears the words of this curse, shall bless himself in his heart, saying, I shall have peace though I walk in the imagination of mine heart, to add drunkenness to thirst, (i. e. run into one debauchery and sin after another:) the Lord will not spare him, but the anger of the Lord, and his jealousy shall smoke against that man;—and the Lord shall separate him unto evil out of all the tribes of Israel, according to all the curses of the covenant, that are written in the book of the law." Deut. xxix. 18–21. There is a terrible emphasis of which we cannot but take notice here: God declares, that if *among all the thousands of Israel*, there was *but one* such presumptuous sinner, that thus *flattered himself in the way of his own heart*, he would make a terrible example of him, and *separate that* one *man to evil*, out of thousands and ten thousands of his faithful and obedient servants.

This therefore is a passage full of apparent terror: the other is indeed a language of mercy; but it contains a most awful insinuation, which appears, as good Archbishop Tillotson expresses it, "like a razor set in oil, which wounds with so much the keener edge." *As I live, saith the Lord God, I have no pleasure in the death of the wicked, but that the wicked turn from his way and live; turn ye, turn ye from your evil ways; for why will ye die, O house of Israel?* (Ezek. xxxiii. 11;) thereby plainly intimating, that notwithstanding all that gentleness of the Divine nature, which he expresses in a most tender invitation, which he confirms even with the solemnity of an oath; yet, if sinners did not *turn from their evil ways*, there was no remedy, but they must *die* for it.

And how, sirs, will any of you that continue in an unregenerate state, arm yourselves against these terrors? Is it by saying, 'that these are the thunders of Mount Sinai; that these are denunciations of the Old Testament; whereas the New speaks in milder language?' You may easily know the contrary.

And to this purpose I am further to show you, that this declaration was renewed by the preaching of *Christ.*

It is true, indeed, that *grace and truth came by Jesus Christ:* (John i. 17:) yet all the grace and gentleness of that adminstration he brought, did not contradict those awful threatenings; nay, it obliged him to set them in a stronger light. He presently repeats to Nicodemus what he had just before asserted in the text, and declares, *Verily, verily, I say unto thee, Except a man be born of water, and of the Spirit, he cannot enter into the kingdom of God;* (John iii. 5;) i. e. 'As he must be baptized with water, in order to a regular entrance into the society of my people, so he must also be transformed by the cleansing and renewing influence of the Spirit, signified by the water there used, or he can have no part in the blessings which my Gospel brings.'

And that this must produce a universal change in the life as well as the heart, and a faithful subjection to the will of God—without which no profession will stand a man in any stead—our Lord solemnly declares in the conclusion of his incomparable discourse on the Mount: "Not every one that saith unto me, Lord, Lord, shall enter into the kingdom of heaven: but he that doth the will of my Father who is in heaven: many will say to me in that day, Lord, Lord, have we not prophesied in thy name, and in thy name cast out devils, and in thy name done many wonderful works? And then will I profess unto them, I never knew you: depart from me, ye that work iniquity." Matt. vii. 21, 22, 23.

And shall you, sirs, merely for having *a name* and *place in his house*, escape; when those that have *preached his Gospel*, and *wrought miracles* in confirmation of it, when those that personally *conversed with Christ*, and those that *ministered unto him* shall perish, if destitute of a holy temper of heart, and of its solid fruit in their lives? Has not our Lord expressly said, that *he will gather out of his kingdom all things that offend, and them that do iniquity; and will cast them into a furnace of fire; there shall be wailing and gnashing of teeth?* Matt. xiii. 41, 42. Nay, in his infinite compassion, he has given to sinners, as it were, a copy of the sentence that will another day be pronounced upon them; that they may meditate upon it, and review it, and judge whether they can bear the terror of its execution. Hear it attentively, and then say whether unregenerate sinners shall *enter into his kingdom.* The dreadful doom is this: *Depart from me, ye cursed, into everlasting fire, prepared for the devil and his angels.* Matt. xxv. 41. And what now will you say to this? Can any soul of you imagine, that the Lord Jesus Christ did not know what would pass in this day in which he is appointed to preside? or that knowing it, and knowing it would be something different from this, he would, on any consideration whatsoever, make a false representation, and lay so much stress upon it? Yet one or other of these things you must secretly imagine; or must own, that every unregenerate sinner, and you among the rest, must not only be excluded from his presence, but be condemned to suffer all the fury of his wrath, in company with devils and damned spirits, in final darkness, and everlasting burning.

It only remains that I show you, that the same testimony was renewed by the *Apostles*, under the influence of the Holy Spirit.

You know that they were authorised by their Great Master to declare, in an authentic manner, the constitution of his kingdom; and that *he who despises them, despises Christ.* Luke x. 16. Now I would fain persuade you all, to consider this argument as it lies in Scripture; to read over the epistolary parts of the New Testament in this view, to observe what encouragement they any of them give to an unregenerate sinner, to expect any part in *the kingdom of heaven.* In the mean time, permit me to present you with a few texts, as a specimen of the rest.

The apostle Paul, in his epistle to the Romans, does indeed speak of God's justifying the *ungodly;* (Rom. iv. 5;) but lest any should vainly imagine that he encourages the hope of those that continue so, he expressly tells us, in the very same epistle, that *the wrath of God is revealed from heaven against all ungodliness and unrighteousness of men;* (Rom. ii. 8;) and that ere long this wrath shall be executed, even in the day of the more ample revelation of the righteous judgment of God; who will render to every man according to his deeds: *To them that do not obey the truth, but obey unrighteousness*, which is the character of every unregenerate sinner, *indignation and wrath: tribulation and anguish upon every soul of man that doth evil, of the Jew first*, as having had the most signal advantages, though advantages inferior to yours, *and also of the Gentile.* Rom. ii. 5, 6, 8, 9. And farther he assures us, that *to be carnally minded is death:* and that *the carnal mind*, which universally prevails in men, till by regenerating grace they are made spiritual, *is enmity against God; for it is not subject to the law of God, neither indeed can be.* Rom. viii. 6, 7.

In another epistle he mentions it as a first principle, in which it might rationally be supposed, no Christian was uninstructed. *Know ye not*, says he, *that the unrighteous shall not inherit the kingdom of God?* 1 Cor. vi. 9. And elsewhere he declares, that all external modes of religion, separate from that entire change of soul which I have described, are worthless and vain. *In Christ*

Jesus, says he, or to those that desire any part in him and his kingdom, *neither circumcision availeth anything, nor uncircumcision, but a new creature.* Gal. vi. 15. He likewise tells us to this purpose in another place, that his grace, which has appeared unto all men, teaches us to deny "ungodliness and worldly lusts, and to live soberly, righteously, and godly in this present world;" (Tit. ii. 11, 12;) and yet, after all, to acknowledge, that it is "not by works of righteousness, which we have done, but according to his mercy he saves us, by the washing of regeneration, and the renewing of the Holy Ghost, which he has shed on us abundantly through Jesus Christ our Saviour." Tit. iii. 5, 6. And *without holiness*, which is the effect of these sacred operations upon the soul, he expressly tells us in another place, that *no man shall see the Lord.* Heb. xii. 14. And to allege but one more passage from him: as it is evident, that all unregenerate sinners, and only they are ignorant of God, and disobedient to the Gospel; he solemnly assures us, that instead of receiving such at last into his kingdom, *the Lord Jesus shall be revealed from heaven, with his mighty angels, in flaming fire, taking vengeance on them that know not God, and that obey not the Gospel of our Lord Jesus Christ: who shall be punished with everlasting destruction from the presence of the Lord, and from the glory of his power.* (2 Thes. i. 7, 8, 9.) This is the testimony of the apostle Paul in his own emphatical words, zealous as he was for the doctrine of free grace, which such declarations as these do not in the least degree contradict.

Let us now hear his brethren, the other apostles of the Lord. James urges sinners, if they ever desire to *draw nigh to God,* and to have him *draw nigh to them,* to *cleanse their hands, and purify their hearts.* James iv. 8. And yet more expressly he says when he speaks of those who should receive the crown of life, which the Lord hath promised to them that love him; *of his own will begat he us with the word of truth, that we should be a kind of first-fruits of his creatures.* Jam. i. 12, 18. The apostle Peter describes Christians, as those whose *souls were purified in obeying the truth through the Spirit—being born again, not of corruptible seed, but of incorruptible;* (1 Pet. i. 22, 23;) and as those who were made *partakers of the Divine Nature, having escaped the corruption that is in the world through lust.* 2 Pet. i. 4. Again, John, the beloved disciple, tells us, that *every one that doth righteousness is born of God;* (1 John ii. 29;) but *he* that *committeth sin is of the devil;* (1 John iii. 8;) and that *every one that has* a well grounded *hope of being like Christ, and seeing him as he is when he appears, purifies himself, even as he is pure.* 1 John iii. 2, 3. And once more, the apostle Jude, as he describes those who are *sensual and have not the Spirit,* as men, that if they were *saved* at all, must be *plucked out of the fire;* (Jude ver. 19, 23 ;) so he echoes back that awful prophecy, which Enoch had so long since delivered, that *the Lord will come with ten thousand of his saints, to execute judgment upon all, and to convict all that are ungodly, of all* those *ungodly deeds and works, by* which they have violated his law. Jude ver. 14, 15.

This then appears, from the whole tenor of the Scriptures, to be the positive and immutable constitution of the great God—that none who are unregenerate shall be admitted to enjoy the happiness of heaven.

And from the view that we have taken of the sacred writings it is manifest, that this, in every age, has been the language of the word of God; and under every dispensation we have sufficient evidence of this important truth. This is the doctrine of the Old Testament; and many are the passages that I have offered from the *law of Moses,* and from *the Prophets,* and the *Psalms,* that show it is impossible an unrenewed soul should enter into heaven. And the same also is asserted in the strongest terms in the New Testament; and when Christ came to set *the Gospel of the kingdom* in a clearer light, the purport of the declaration that he makes to Nicodemus in the text, was frequently repeated by him in the course of his preaching, and represented as the rule he would regard at the last day. And the inspired apostles speak the same thing with a united voice, and testify at large in their epistles, that it is absolutely necessary we should *be born again,* if ever we would hope to *see the kingdom of God.*

So that now, sirs, I may say, *Call, if there be any that will answer; and to which of the saints will you turn,* (Job v. 1,) to encourage your vain and presumptuous hope, of finding your lot among God's people in the kingdom of glory, if you are strangers to that important and universal change, which we before described as *regeneration* in the Scripture sense of the word? The prophets under the Old Testament, and Christ and his apostles under the New, concur, in all the variety of the most awful language, to expose so presumptuous a hope. And is it not audacious madness in any to venture their souls upon it? Thus you would undoubtedly judge of any man who should strike a dagger into his breast, or discharge a pistol at his head, on this presumption, that the almighty power of God could prevent his death, though the heart or the brain were pierced.

But it is much greater folly for a man, while he continues in an unregenerate state, to promise himself a part in the kingdom of heaven. For though there would be no reason in the world to expect a miraculous interposition, to save a life which a man was so resolutely bent to destroy; yet none can say, that such an interposition would contradict any of the express engagements of God's word; whereas to admit an unregenerate sinner into the regions of glory, would be violating, not *this*, or *that* single declaration, but the whole series and tenor of it; and we shall farther show, in the next Discourse, that it would also be, in effect, altering the very nature of the heavenly kingdom itself, as well as its constitution. Now what hope can be more desperate, than that which can have no support, but in the subversion of the Redeemer's kingdom, and even of the eternal throne of God, the foundations of which are righteousness and truth!

DISCOURSE V.

OF THE INCAPACITY OF AN UNREGENERATE PERSON FOR RELISHING THE ENJOYMENTS OF THE HEAVENLY WORLD.

JOHN III. 3.

—Except a man be born again, he can not see the kingdom of God.

In order to demonstrate the necessity of regeneration, of which I would fain convince not only your understandings, but your consciences, I am now proving to you, that without it, it is impossible to enter into the kingdom of God; and how weighty a consideration that is I am afterwards to represent.

That it is thus impossible, the words in the text do indeed sufficiently prove: but for the further illustration of the subject, I have proposed to consider it under two distinct views.

I have already shown it is impossible, because the constitution of the kingdom of heaven is such, that God has solemnly declared, and this under different dispensations, and more or less plainly in all ages of his church, that no unregenerate person, i. e. no impenitent sinner, shall have any part in it. And I am now further to show,

That the *nature* of the *future happiness*, which is here chiefly signified by *the kingdom of God*, is such, that an unregenerate person would be incapable of relishing it, even upon a supposition of his being admitted into it.

This is a thought of so great importance, and so seldom represented in its full strength, that I shall at present confine my discourse entirely to it.

I know, sinners, it will be one of the most difficult things in the world, to bring you to a serious persuasion of this truth. You think heaven is so lovely, and so glorious a place, that if you could possibly get an admittance there, you should certainly be happy. But I would now set myself, if possible, to convince you that this is a rash and ill-grounded persuasion; and that on the contrary, if you were now in the regions of glory, and in the society of those blessed inhabitants, that unrenewed nature and unsanctified heart of yours, would give you a disrelish for all the sublimest entertainments of that blissful place, and turn heaven itself into a kind of hell to you.

Now for the demonstration of this, it is only

necessary for you seriously to consider what kind of happiness that of heaven is, as it is represented to us in the word of God; for from thence undoubtedly we are to take our notions of it.

You might to be sure sit down and imagine a happiness to yourselves, which would perfectly suit your degenerate taste; a happiness, which the more entirely you were enslaved to flesh and sense, the more exquisitely you would be able to enter into it. If God would assign you a region in that beautiful world, where you should dwell in fine houses magnificently furnished, and gaily adorned; where the most harmonious music should soothe your ear, and the most delicious food and generous wines in a rich variety should regale your taste: if he should give you a splendid retinue of people, to caress and attend you, offering you their humblest services, and acknowledging the most servile dependence upon your favor: especially if with all this he should furnish you with a set of companions just of your own temper and disposition, with whom you might spend what proportion of time you pleased, in gaming and jollity, in riot and debauchery, without any interruption from the reproof, or even the example of the children of God, or from indispositions of body, or remorse of conscience: this you would be ready to call life and happiness indeed: and if the great Disposer of all things were but to add perpetuity to such a situation, you would not envy persons of a more refined taste the heaven you lost, for such a Paradise as this.

Such indeed was the happiness which Mahomet promised to his followers: flowery shades and gay dresses, luxurious fare and beautiful women, are described with all the pomp of language in almost every page of his Alcoran, as the glorious and charming rewards which were to be bestowed on the faithful after the resurrection. And if this were the felicity which the Gospel promised, extortioners and idolators, whoremongers and drunkards, would be much fitter to *inherit the kingdom of God*, than the most pious and mortified saints that ever appeared on earth. But here, as almost everywhere else, the Bible and the Alcoran speak a very different language; and far from leading us into such gross and sensual expectations, our Lord Jesus Christ has told us that *the children of the resurrection neither marry, nor are given in marriage; but are like the angels of God in heaven,* (Matt. xxii. 30,) and enjoy such pure and spiritual delights, as are suited to such holy and excellent creatures.

It is true that in the book of Revelations, stately palaces and shining habits, delicious fruit and harmonious music are all mentioned, as contributing to the happiness of those, who have the honor to inhabit the New Jerusalem. But then the style of that obscure and prophetical book naturally leads us to consider these merely as figurative phrases, which are made use of to express the happiness that Divine wisdom and love has prepared for the righteous, in a manner accommodated to the weakness of our conceptions; or at least, if in any of these respects provision be made for the entertainment of a *glorified body*, whatever its methods of sensation and perception will be, all will be temperate and regular; and after all, this is *even there* represented but as the least considerable part of our happiness, the height of which is made to consist in the most elevated strains of devotion, and in an entire and everlasting devotedness to the service of God and of the Lamb.

Let us therefore immediately proceed to settle the point in question, by a more particular survey of the several branches of the celestial felicity, as represented to us in the word of God; and from thence it will undeniably appear, that were an unregenerate soul in the same place with the blessed, and surrounded with the same external circumstances, the temper of the mind would not by any means allow him to participate of their happiness. For it is plain the Scripture represents the happiness of heaven as consisting,—in the perfection of our minds in knowledge and holiness;—in the sight and service of the ever blessed God,—in beholding the glory of our exalted Redeemer;—and enjoying the society of glorious angels and perfected saints,—throughout an endless eternity. Now, sinners, it is impossible you should enter into any such delights as these, while you continue in an unregenerate state.

1. One very considerable part of the happiness of heaven consists in that perfection of knowledge and holiness to which the blessed shall be there exalted; but in which the unregenerate soul can have no pleasure.

Thus we are told, that *the spirits of just men* shall there be *made perfect;* (Heb. xiii. 23;) for *nothing that defiles,* as every degree of moral imperfection does, *shall enter into the New Jerusalem.* Rev. xxi. 27. An Old Testament saint conceived of future happiness, as consisting in *being satisfied with the likeness of God:* (Psal. xvii. 15;) a character that is manifestly most agreeable to the view of it, which the beloved disciple gives us, where he says, that *when Christ shall appear, we shall be like him, for we shall see him as he is;* (1 John iii. 2;) which must certainly refer to the glories of the mind, which are of infinitely greater importance than the highest imaginable beauty and ornament, that can be put upon the corporeal part of our nature in its most illustrious state.

Now from this perfection and holiness, which shall then be wrought in the soul, there will naturally arise an unspeakable complacency and joy, something resembling that which the blessed God himself possesses, in the survey of the infinite and unspotted rectitude of his own most holy nature. And in proportion to the degree, in which *the eyes of our understandings are enlightened* to discern wherein true excellency consists, will the soul be delighted in the consciousness of such considerable degrees of it in itself.

But surely it will be superfluous for me to undertake to demonstrate, that an unregenerate soul can have no part in this divine pleasure, which implies the complete renewal of the mind as its very foundation. For to imagine that he might, would be supposing him regenerate and unregenerate at the same time. As Mr. Baxter very well expresses it, "The happiness of heaven is holiness; and to talk of being happy without it is as apparent nonsense, as to talk of being well without health, or being saved without salvation."

I would only add on this head, that the highest improvement of our intellectual faculties could not make us happy, without such a change in the affections and the will, as I have before described under the former general head. For the more clear and distinct the knowledge of true excellence and perfection is, the greater would be your anguish and horror, to see and feel yourselves entirely destitute of it; and it is exceedingly probable that spirits of the most elevated genius have the keenest sensation of that infamy and misery, which is inseparable from the prevalence of sinful dispositions in such minds as these.

2. Another very considerable branch of the celestial happiness, is that which arises, from the contemplation and enjoyment of the ever blessed God; but of this likewise an unregenerate sinner is incapable.

As our own reason assures us, that God is the greatest and best of beings, and the most deserving object of our inquiries and regards, one would think it would naturally lead us to imagine, that the perfection and happiness of the human soul consists in the knowledge and enjoyment of him; and that when it arrives at the seat of complete felicity, it must intimately know him, and converse with him. And in this view, I have sometimes been surprised, that men of such distinguished abilities, as some of the heathen poets and philosophers appear to have been, should have had no greater regard to the Supreme Being in the description which they give us of the future happiness. That sort of friendship for them, which an acquaintance with their writings must give to a person of any relish for the beauties of composition, makes one almost unwilling to expose the low and despicable ideas, which they often give of the state of their greatest heroes in the regions of immortality. But the word of God speaks a very different language. Our Lord represents the rewards to be bestowed on the *pure in heart,* by telling us *that they shall see,* i. e. contemplate and enjoy *God;* (Matt. v. 8 ;) and virtuous souls who overcome the temptations with which they are here surrounded, shall be *made as pillars in the house of their God, and shall go no more out:* (Rev. iii. 12 ;) and it is elsewhere said that *his servants shall serve him, and shall see his face.* Rev. xxii. 3, 4. And David's views under a darker dispensation rose to such a degree of refinement, as to say, *As for me, I shall behold thy face in righteousness;* (Psal. xvii. 1 ;) which he mentions as a felicity infinitely superior to all the delights of the most prosperous sinner.

But now, sinners, it is utterly impossible that while you continue in an unregenerate state, you should *behold the face of God* with pleasure. The unutterable delight which the blessed inhabitants of heaven find in it, arises not merely from the abstract ideas of his essential perfections, but from a sense of his favor and love to them. It is this that gives a relish to the whole survey, and rejoices the heart of all the saints, both in heaven and on earth. He is a God of awful majesty and irresistible power, of infinite wisdom and unspotted holiness, of unerring justice, invariable fidelity, and inexhaustible goodness; and *this God is our God; he will be our guide and our portion forever.* Psal. xlviii. 14; lxxiii. 26. And were it not for this view, let a creature think of God with ever so much spirit and propriety, he must *think of him, and be troubled;* (Psal. lxxvii. 3;) yea, he must be filled with unutterable horror and confusion, as the devil is at the thought of an infinitely perfect Being, in whom he has no interest, from whom he has nothing friendly to expect; and if nothing friendly, then everything dreadful.

Now it is certain, sinners, that while you continue in an unregenerate state, under the influence of that *carnal mind* which *is enmity against God,* (Rom. viii. 7,) and full of unconquerable rebellion against his law, there can be no foundation for a friendship between him and your souls; nor for any persuasion, or any apprehension of your interest in his favor and love. Friendship, you know, supposes something of a similitude of nature and sentiment; for as God himself argues, *how can two walk together except they be agreed?* Amos iii. 3. Now I have before observed to you at large, that *God* being *of purer eyes than to behold evil,* (Heb. i. 13,) must necessarily *hate all the workers of iniquity; the foolish therefore shall not stand in his sight,* (Psal. v. 5,) or shall not be admitted to such a situation: nor would they indeed be able to endure it. Let conscience judge what satisfaction you could find in the presence of a God, that you knew scorned and hated you, even while he suffered you to continue among the crowd of his children and servants. The more lively ideas you had of the beauty and perfection of the Divine nature, the more you must *loathe yourselves* for being so unlike him, and so abominable to him: and what pleasure do you think consistent with such self-contempt and abhorrence? Or rather, would not the wretched degeneracy of your nature lead you another way; and a kind of unconquerable self-love, joined even with this consciousness of deformity and vileness, lead you to hate God himself? It is described as the fatal effect of prevailing wickedness in the heart, *my soul loathed them, and their soul also abhorred me.* Zechariah xi. 8. And thus would it probably work in you, and produce in your wretched breasts a mortal hatred against him, and an envious rage at the thought of his perfect happiness; a state of mind, of all others that can be imagined, the most odious, and the most tormenting.

How, sirs, could your hearts, possessed with these diabolical passions, bear to see the beams of his glory surrounding you on every side? How could you bear to hear the songs and adorations, that were continually addressed to his throne; and to observe the humble attendance of all the hosts of heaven about it, who perpetually reckon it their honor and happiness to be employed in obedience to his commands? Such a sight of the glory and felicity of your Divine Enemy would make you, so far as your limited nature was capable of it, miserable even in proportion to the degree in which he is happy. This was, no doubt, the torment of the devils as soon as they had harbored a thought of hostility against God; and the remembrance of that glory in which they once saw him, and which they know he still invariably possesses, is surely an everlasting vexation to them: and it would be so to you, if you were within the sight of it.

But further, the blessed in heaven find their everlasting entertainment in the *service* of God. *They rest not day and night, saying, Holy, holy, holy, Lord God Almighty;* (Rev. iv. 8;) i. e. they are continually employed, either in the immediate acts of devotion, or in other services, in which they still maintain a devotional temper, and are breathing out their souls in holy affections, while their active powers are employed in the execution of his commands. But as I have already shown you, that while in an unregenerate state you could have no sense of his favor to you, it is very apparent, that you could have no sentiments of gratitude and love towards him. So that while angels and glorified saints were breathing out their souls in the most delightful and rapturons praises, you must keep a sullen silence; or, if it were possible that your harps and voices should sound as melodiously as theirs, it would be all ceremony and show; the music of the heart would be wanting; and you would look on all the external forms of service but as a tedious task, and count it your misfortune, that the customs of the place obliged you to attend them.

You may the more easily apprehend and believe this when you consider what little relish you now have for those solemnities of Divine worship, in which sincere Christians have the most lively foretaste of heaven. You know, in your own consciences, that short and interrupted as our public services are, they are the burden of your lives. You know that you say, in your hearts at least,

When will the Sabbath be past, and the new moon be gone? Amos viii. Judge then how insupportable it would be to you, to spend an everlasting Sabbath thus. I question not, but to your wretched spirits annihilation would appear vastly preferable to an eternal existence so employed.

3. Another very considerable branch of the happiness of heaven, is that which arises from the sight of the glory of an exalted *Redeemer;* but for this likewise no unconverted sinner can have any relish.

This is a view of the future happiness, which our Lord gives us, when he prays for his people in those memorable words, engraven, as I hope, upon many of our hearts; *Father, I will that they whom thou hast given me, be with me where I am, that they may behold my glory which thou hast given me.* John xvii. 24. And he elsewhere promises it, as the great reward he would bestow upon his people; *If any man serve me, let him follow me; and where I am, there also shall my servant be.* John xii. 26. And agreeably to this, the apostle Paul represents it as the transporting view in which he considered the happiness of the future world; *I desire,* says he, *to depart and be with Christ; which is far better;* (Phil. i. 28;) incomparably beyond any of the enjoyments of the present world which can come into competition with it. But for *this part* of the happiness of angels, and of *the spirits of just men made perfect,* it is also evident, that you, sinners, can have no relish.

The sight of Christ will afford holy souls a transporting delight, because they will regard it as the glory of their Redeemer and their Friend, and as a pledge and security of their own glory. But what foundation can you, sinners, find for such a joyful sympathy with Christ, and such a comfortable conclusion with regard to yourselves? Such is the wretched degeneracy of your nature, that though Christ be indeed *the chiefest among ten thousand,* and *altogether lovely,* (Cant. v. 10, 16.) being *the brightness of* his Father's *glory, and the express image of his person,* (Heb. i. 3,) possessed of every divine perfection and excellence; yet you now slight and neglect him, and discern in him *no form or comeliness, for which he is to be desired:* (Isa. liii. 2:) and were you unregenerate in heaven, the same principle would prevail. Now where there is no love to a person, there can be no delight in his converse, nor any pleasure in his happiness. Nay, the contrariety of your nature to his would rather occasion aversion and terror. You could not but know, that the blessed Jesus is holy and undefiled, and *separate from sinners;* (Heb. vii. 26;) that he abhors all moral evil to such a degree, that he laid aside all the glory and entertainments of heaven, that he might destroy the interest of sin in this world of ours, and might *purify to himself a peculiar people, zealous of good works:* (Tit. ii. 14 :) and when you should recollect at the same time that sinfulness that continued to reign in your hearts, and made you to *every good work reprobate,* (Tit. i. 16,) you could not but know that you must be hateful to him; and therefore could not but fear, lest his almighty power should be exercised for your punishment and destruction: and thus your terror must rise, in proportion to the sensible evidence you had of his dignity and authority. In a word, you would stand like guilty rebels in the presence-chamber of their injured and displeased Sovereign: his throne and his sceptre, his robe and his crown, his courtiers and his guards, though in themselves splendid and magnificent objects, only serve to terrify and amaze them, while they display the grandeur and power of their enemy.

4. Another very considerable branch of the celestial happiness will be the society of angels and glorified saints; but for this likewise an unregenerate sinner must be unfit.

You know that when the apostle speaks of our alliance to the heavenly world, he represents it as a social state; where excellent spirits dwell together, and converse with each other with mutual esteem and endearment: *ye are come*, says he, *to the heavenly Jerusalem, and to an innumerable company of angels, to the general assembly and church of the first-born, which are written in heaven, and to the spirits of just men made perfect.* Heb. xii. 22, 23. It is *sitting down with Abraham, Isaac, and Jacob*, with all the patriarchs and prophets, all the apostles and martyrs *in the kingdom of heaven:* (Matt. viii. 11 :) and perhaps you think you shall want nothing more to complete your happiness, than to be admitted to a place among them. But reflect a little more attentively upon the circumstances of things, and I am persuaded you will form a different judgment.

There is no reason to doubt, but that at your first entrance into the regions of glory you would be agreeably struck with the view of those inhabitants. As for those beauties of their character, which consist in love to God, and in zeal for his honor and interest, it is certain, that you would be insensible of them, and pay but little regard to them: but the humanity and benevolence of their temper would, no doubt, render them agreeable to you; and so much the more, as self-love might lead you to expect some personal advantage by it. And it is more than possible, that you would be much prejudiced in their favor by those resplendent and attractive forms in which they appear; forms, no doubt, far more beautiful and engaging than any which the children of men ever saw upon earth. On both these accounts it might be natural enough for you, at first, to address them with an air of respect, as persons that you could be glad to be upon good terms with, and in whose friendship you could desire a share.

But how do you think that any such proposal of friendship would be received by an angel, or a glorified saint? No doubt, if there were any prospect of converting you, or any hope you might be brought to a devout and holy temper, they would immediately become *preachers of righteousness* to you; and endeavor by the most rational, the most pathetic, and the most insinuating address, to awaken and charm you to a sense of religion, and so to form you to a capacity for happiness. But they would know, that according to the eternal constitution of God, there could be no room to entertain such a hope; but that *being filthy*, you must be *filthy still:* (Rev. xxii. 11:) and therefore, as they would know you to be incorrigible, their love to God, and their concern to be approved and accepted by him, would prevent their forming any intimate friendship with persons whose natures were so contrary to him, and on whom he looked with such irreconcilable abhorrrence. And besides this, their own personal sanctity of character would give them an aversion to such corrupt and degenerate creatures: so that how much soever they might pity your condition, they would turn away from you, as objects whose presence and converse were not to be endured.

And do you not easily apprehend, that such a refusal on their part would be both shameful and very provoking to you? For which way could you bear it, to be thus rejected and dishonored by the most excellent part of the creation; by those whom perhaps you once intimately knew, and with whom you conversed upon equal terms; nay, by many who were once much your inferiors, and whom, perhaps, in the pride of your hearts, you would not condescend to regard? The natural effect of this must surely be, that you would soon be proportionably displeased and enraged with the refusal, as you were at first charmed at their appearance; and when you saw that transporting pleasure which they took in the affection and friendship of each other, and the joy which the Divine favor poured into their souls, while you, in the very same place, were excluded from these rich entertainments, your hearts would soon burn with envy and indignation; and as much as you before admired them, you, upon this, would come to hate them. And, perhaps, that hatred would put you upon some attempt to interrupt, or even, if it were possible, to destroy that happiness which you were not allowed to share. But, then, when you saw them continually under the Divine protection, and *compassed with his favor as with a shield*, (Psalm v. 12,) so that your malice could not reach them, all the keenness and rancor of your spirit would recoil upon itself; you would fly from their presence, as insupportable; and would be glad to retire to some meaner apartment, or to hide yourselves in the shades of darkness; so that you might but get rid of the sight of so many dazzling objects, whose lustre, instead of cheering your vitiated eye, would pain and overpower it.

But if you should not be transported to this diabolical excess—if it were possible for you to behold the glorified saints, and to live among them, without these envious and tormenting passions; yet surely you would want a relish for the most entertaining part of their conversation. Had you indeed a good natural genius, which to be sure many unconverted sinners have, it might be very agreeable to hear them discoursing of the wonders of nature; and that curiosity, which is in some measure incident even to persons of the meanest capacities, would make it pleasant to hear them recount the important history relating to the revolutions of the angelic world, which we on this earth are entirely strangers to, or at least have been very little acquainted with them. But surely the most delightful topics of conversation, which heaven itself can furnish out, must be those which are religious and divine; the infinite perfections of the ever blessed God; the personal glories and incomparable love of his condescending, but exalted Son; and the sanctifying operations of the blessed Spirit on the soul, transforming it into the Divine Image, and making it meet for eternal glory. Yes, even when the blessed spirits above are handling philosophical or historical subjects, they still consider them with a regard to God, as his perfections are displayed and illustrated in the works of his hands, and in the conduct of his providence. And here their pleasure flows, not merely from a set of rational ideas, which arise in their own minds, or are suggested to them by others: but from the exercise of those devout affections upon the blessed God, which are correspondent to these several subjects of discourse.

And can you, sirs, who are *alienated from the*

divine life, (Eph. iv. 18,) and accustomed to live in a continual neglect and forgetfulness of the Great Parent of universal nature, can you relish such subjects as these? You would, no doubt, be discontented and uneasy in such a scene: the heavenly oratory of this holy society would have no charms for you; but you would be longing for some of those vain and worthless companions, whom you were so fond of here upon earth, to hear a merry story, or a song, or to join with them in the pleasures of a debauch.

5. Another considerable branch of the happiness of heaven arises from the assured prospect of the *everlasting continuance* of this felicity; but, if an unregenerate soul could find any entertainment at all in heaven, he certainly could have no ground for such an expectation of its continuance.

When the children of God on earth think of the happiness of heaven, the eternity of it makes a very deep impression on their hearts, and even swallows up their souls with ardent desire and unutterable joy: it raises their esteem, and animates their hope, while they reflect on that *exceeding and eternal weight of glory*, (2 Cor. iv. 17,) that *house not made with hands, eternal in the heavens*, (2 Cor. v. 1,) and that *inheritance incorruptible and undefiled, and which fadeth not away*. 1 Pet. i. 4. And no doubt that the blessed in heaven regard it in the same view, and all the pleasures they enjoy are vastly increased by the prospect of their endless duration; so that by the anticipation of an eternity still to come, they do, as it were, every moment enjoy an infinite satisfaction. But as for you, sinners, while you are so ill attempered to the happiness of heaven, the prospect of an eternal abode there would not, on the principles I have laid down above, be a prospect of eternal happiness, but rather, on the whole, of eternal uneasiness to you.

But suffer me a little to discourse upon another supposition; and let me now, for argument sake, waive what I have been so long insisting upon, and suppose, that you could so far command the turbulent passions of your own heart, and so unite, as it were, the whole powers of your soul, to attend to the beauty of place, the harmony of music, and whatever else may be supposed capable of regaling the senses or the imagination, as upon the whole, to find heaven a pleasing and delightful abode, and to wish, that though some of its entertainments were above your taste and capacity, yet you might be allowed an eternal enjoyment of the rest; could there be any room for you to expect a perpetual abode in these blissful seats? No, sinners, you would not be able so much as to hope it. The good itself is so great, and perpetual enjoyment, even in any degree, has such a kind of infinite value, that I know not how the purest and noblest spirits in heaven could absolutely have been secure of it, separate from the engagement of a Divine promise.

And what Divine promise would you be able to have recourse to in such a circumstance as we now suppose? Where could you find it in all the book of God, that persons of your character should ever enter into heaven at all, much less that you should forever continue there? You could have therefore no security of the continuance of your abode in heaven, if it were possible that you should enter on the possession of it: but when you should consider the unsullied holiness of the ever blessed God, the sovereign of this sacred province, and the spotless purity of that gracious Redeemer, to whom the government of it is committed, you could not but fear, that you should quickly be seized by the hand of vengeance, be hurled from the battlements of heaven, and plunged low into the pit of destruction. You know this was the condemnation of the rebel angels, and your guilt, compared with that dreadful event, which makes so considerable a scene of the history of heaven, would, I doubt not, be sufficient to create everlasting jealousy and uneasiness, and to turn every pleasurable circumstance into a source of horror, in the apprehensions of being deprived eternally of it.

Thus you see, sirs, from a particular survey of the various lights in which heaven is represented, and of the various branches of which its happiness consists, an unregenerate sinner is incapable of it, even though we would suppose that he was actually admitted to it. Let me entreat you to reflect on all these things, and you will see the reasonableness of that one remark with which I shall conclude this discourse, viz.:

How vain are all those hopes of heaven, which in your present condition you are ready to entertain!

I have been proving at large, that if God were to admit you to the possession of heaven, which it is certain he never will, you would be incapable of relishing the enjoyment of it: nay, that there would be a solid foundation in your own hearts, for many of the most tumultuous and disquieting passions. Envy and grief, fear and rage, those roots of bitterness, would spring up even in the Paradise of God, and turn the fertility of that blessed soil into their own nourishment. And do you imagine that any external accommodations or ornaments could make you easy and comfortable, under the transports of such hellish passions? What if you were to take a man that was tormented with a violent fit of the stone or gout, and to place him in a most delicious garden, or in a palace of marble and cedar, to set him on a throne of gold under a canopy of purple, to clothe him with robes of velvet and embroidery, regaling him with the most delicious fruits and generous wines, and at the same time soothing his ear with all the harmony of sound, which the most melodious symphony of instruments and voices could afford? Would all this magnificence and luxury make him insensible of that anguish which was racking his very vitals? or would not that inward torture rather render him insensible of this association of pleasurable impressions from without? Yea, would it not incline him to suspect, that you intended all these pompous preparations only to deride and insult him? As little would your distempered and unholy souls be capable of relishing the entertainments of heaven, while these entertainments and these souls of yours, continue what they are at present.

There *must* be therefore a change: and will you consider where that change must be made? If you continue still in your present character and circumstances, there must be a vast change in heaven itself, before you can be happy in it. The whole temper, character, and disposition of every saint and angel there, must be changed from what it now is, before they can be capable of any friendly and complacential conversation with you. Yea, our Lord Jesus Christ, who is *the same yesterday, to-day, and forever*, (Heb. xiii. 9,) must divest himself of those beauties of holiness, which are infinitely dearer to him than any external grandeur or authority, before he can receive you into his kingdom. Nay, the very *Father of lights, with whom there is no variableness, neither shadow of turning*, (Jam. i. 17,) must be entirely changed. He must lay aside that holiness which is essential to his nature, and which is the brightness and glory of it: he must love that which he now hates, and be indifferent to that which he most affectionately loves, before he can open his arms to you, and smile upon your souls. And can you dare to hope for such an unaccountable, such an inconceivable revolution as this? No, sirs, infinitely sooner would God change earth into hell, and bury you, and all of your character, under the ruins of this world, which you inhabit and pollute, than he would thus tarnish the beauties of heaven, and divest himself of the brightest glory of his own divinity. "God," says Archbishop Tillotson, "has condescended to take our nature upon him, that he might make us capable of happiness; but if this will not do, he will not put off his own nature to make us happy."

What then do you imagine? Do you think that God will prepare some separate apartments in heaven, furnished with a variety of sensual pleasures, for the entertainment of persons of your character? some apartments from whence the tokens of his presence shall be withdrawn, from whence the exercise of his worship shall be banished, from whence saints and angels shall retire to make way for those inhabitants, who, like you, have sinned themselves beyond a capacity of enjoying God, or of being fit companions for any of his most excellent creatures? This were to suppose the Christian religion false, and to contradict the light of natural reason too, which not only shows such a disposition of things to be unworthy the Divine sanctity and majesty, but also shows that if there be a future state, it must be a state of misery to wicked men, in whose minds those vicious habits prevail, which are even now the beginnings of hell; which therefore they must carry along with them wherever they are, in proportion to the degree in which they are predominant.

Upon the whole then, you must evidently see that it is absolutely necessary that you, sinners, should be changed, if ever you expect to have any part or lot in the future happiness. And when do you expect that change should be wrought?

Do you expect it when death has done its dreadful office upon you, and your soul arrives at the invisible world? Is the air of it, if I may be allowed the expression, so refined that it will immediately purify, and transform every polluted sinner that comes into it? You cannot but know, that the whole tenor of scripture forbids that presumptuous destructive hope. It assures us that *there is no work, nor device, nor knowledge, nor wisdom in the grave;* (Eccl. ix. 10;) but that we must be *judged according to what we have done in the body*, and not according to what has passed in a separate state, *whether* the actions we have done be *good, or* whether they be *evil.* 2 Cor. v. 10.

If ever therefore you are regenerate at all, it must be while you are here below, in this state of education and trial: and if you continue in your sins till death surprise you, your souls will be forever sealed up under an irreversible sentence, and by the decree of God, and the constitution of things, will be excluded from happiness, as by no means either entitled to it, or prepared for it. So evident is the truth of this assertion in the text, that *Except a man be born again he cannot see the kingdom of God.*

And will you then sit down contentedly under such conclusion as this, "I shall be excluded from this kingdom, as accursed and profane?" Alas, sirs, the conclusion is big with unutterable terror and death, as I should now proceed to show you at large if my time would allow: for I am next to represent the infinite importance of entering into that kingdom, and consequently of that entire change which has been proved to be necessary to that entrance. But I must reserve that to the next opportunity of this kind.

In the mean time let me add, that I doubt not but there are many present, who have heard this description of the heavenly world with delight, and who are saying in their hearts, "*This is my rest forever: here will I dwell, for I have desired it:* (Psal. cxxxii. 14:) This is the felicity to which my heart aspires with the most ardent breathing." Such may with the utmost reason regard it as a token for good, and may go on in a cheerful assurance, that the grace that has *made them meet to be partakers of the inheritance of the saints in light,* (Col. i. 12,) will at length conduct them to it, in perfect safety and everlasting triumph. *Amen.*

DISCOURSE VI.

OF THE IMPORTANCE OF ENTERING INTO THE KINGDOM OF HEAVEN

JOHN III. 3.

—Except a man be born again, he can not see the kingdom of God.

How impossible it is that an unregenerate sinner should *see the kingdom of God*, or enjoy that future blessedness to which the Gospel is intended to lead its professors, I have shown you at large. I have appealed to the testimony of God's holy prophets, and apostles, in concurrence with that of his incarnate Son, to prove that persons of such a character are, by the inviolable constitution of that kingdom, excluded from it. And I have further, in my last discourse, proved, that if they were actually admitted to it, they would be incapable of relishing its pleasures: that their vitiated palate would have a distaste to the choicest fruits of the Paradise of God; yea, that in these blessed regions thorns and briers would spring up in their paths, and make them wretched in the very seat of happiness.

I doubt not, but you are in your consciences generally convinced, that the truth of these things cannot be contested. You are inwardly persuaded that it is indeed so; and I fear many of you have also reason to apprehend, that you are of this unhappy number, who are hitherto strangers to regenerating grace. But how are your minds impressed with this apprehension? Do I wrong you, sirs, when I suspect that some of you are hardly impressed at all? Do I wrong you when I suspect there are those of you, who have spent the last week with very little reflection upon what you have heard? The cares and amusements of life have been pursued as before, and you have not taken one hour to enter into the thought with self-application, and seriously to consider, 'I am one of these concerning whom eternal wisdom and truth has pronounced, that if they continue such as at present they are, they *shall not see the kingdom of heaven.*' You have not paused at all upon the awful thought; you have not offered one lively petition to God, to beg that you may be recovered from this unhappy state, and brought to a meetness for his kingdom, and a title to it. For your sakes therefore, and for the sakes of others in your state, having already explained, illustrated, and confirmed the proposition in my text, I proceed,

III. To represent to you the IMPORTANCE of the argument suggested here; or to show you how much every unregenerate sinner ought to be alarmed to hear, that while he continues in his present state, *he cannot see the kingdom of God.*

And oh! that while I endeavor to illustrate this, my words might enter into your minds, *as goads*, and might fix there *as nails fastened in a sure place!* The substance of my argument is *given forth by* the *one* great *Shepherd;* (Eccles. xii. 11;) may the prosecution of it be blessed, as the means of reducing some wandering sheep into his fold.

Now in order to illustrate the force of this argument, I beseech you seriously to consider,—what this kingdom is, from which you are in danger of being forever excluded:—and what will be the condition of all those, who shall be finally cut off from any interest in it.

Consider first *what that kingdom is*, from which the unregenerate, or those who are not born again, shall be excluded.

And here you are not to expect a complete representation of it: for that is an attempt in which the tongues of angels, as well as men, might fail; or how proper soever their language might be in itself, to us it would be unintelligible: for *eye hath not seen, nor ear heard, neither have entered into the heart of man, the things which God hath prepared for them that love him.* 1 Cor. ii. 9. And surely these final and most illustrious preparations of his love must, beyond all others, exceed our description and conception. A minister, that, with the apostle Paul, had been *caught up into the third heaven,* if he would attempt to speak of the glorious scenes which were there opened to him, must say, they were *unutterable things:* (2 Cor. xii. 2, 4:) and one, that with John, had *lain in the bosom of Christ* himself, must say, as that Apostle did, *It does not yet appear what we shall be.* 1 John iii. 2. And indeed, when we go about to discourse of it, I doubt not but the blessed angels pity the weakness of our apprehensions and expressions, and know that we do but debase the subject, when we attempt the most to exalt and adorn it.

Yet there are just and striking representations of this kingdom made in the word of God; and we are there often told in general, wherein it shall consist. You no doubt remember that I was, in the last of these Lectures, going over several important views of it. I then told you, it will consist in the perfection of our souls in knowledge and holiness; in the sight of God and our blessed

Redeemer; in exercising the most delightful affections towards them, and in being forever employed in rendering them the most honorable services; in conversing with saints and glorious angels; and in the assured expectation of the eternal continuance of this blessedness in all its branches. That this is the scriptural representation of the matter, I proved to you from many express testimonies in the word of God; and I doubt not, but you have often heard the excellency of each of these views represented at large, in distinct discourses on each.

I will not therefore now repeat what has been said upon such occasions; but will rather direct you to some general considerations, which may convince you of the excellency of that state and world, from which, if you continue unregenerate, you must forever be excluded: for I would fain fix it upon your minds, that it is in this connection, and for this purpose, that the representation is made. And oh! that you might so review it, as no longer to *neglect so great salvation*, (Heb. ii. 3,) nor act as if you *judged* such *everlasting life* to be beneath your attention, and *unworthy* your care and regard! Acts xiii. 46. You cannot think it so when you consider,—that it is represented in scripture under the most magnificent images;—that it is the state which God has prepared for the display of his glory, and the entertainment of his most favorite creatures; that it is the purchase of the blood of his eternal Son, that it is the main work of his sacred Spirit to prepare men's hearts for it; and the great business of our inveterate enemy, the devil, by all possible means, to prevent our obtaining it. Each of these considerations may much illustrate the excellency of it and all taken together yield a most convincing demonstration.

1. Consider, by what a variety of beautiful and magnificent images this happiness is represented in the word of God; and that may convince you of its excellency.

When the blessed God himself would raise our conceptions of a state of being, so much superior to anything we have ever seen or known, unless he intended a personal and miraculous revelation of it, he must borrow our language, and in painting the glory of heaven must take his colors from earth. And here the magnificence of a city, the sweetness of a garden, the solemn pomp of a temple, the lustre of a crown, and the dignity of a kingdom, strike powerfully on the human mind, and fill it with veneration and delight. But when such figures as these are borrowed from this lower world of ours, faintly to shadow out that which is above, there is always the addition of some important circumstance, to intimate how far the celestial original exceeds the brightest earthly glory, by which the Divine condescension has vouchsafed to describe it.

The enumeration of a variety of scriptural descriptions will set these remarks in the strongest light. If therefore heaven be described as a city, it is *the New Jerusalem, the city of our God, that cometh down from God out of heaven;* (Rev. iii. 12, xxi. 2;) the pavement of its *streets* is all of *pure gold,* its *gates* are *pearl,* and its *foundations jewels.* Rev. xxi. 19, 21. If it be a garden, it is the *Paradise of God,* (Rev. ii. 7,) and so far superior to that which he at first prepared and furnished out for the entertainment of Adam in his state of innocence, that it is *planted* on *every side* with *the tree of life,* (Rev. xxii. 2,) of which there was but one alone in the garden of Eden: and is watered, not with such common rivers as the Tigris and Euphrates, but with that living, copious, inexhausted stream, *the river of the water of life,* which *proceeds from the throne of God,* (Rev. xxii. 1,) and gently glides along through all its borders. When it is represented as a temple, we are told that instead of a golden ark placed in the remotest recess, to which only the high priest might once a year approach, and on which he might not be allowed to gaze, the *throne of God* is erected *there*, (Rev. vii. 15,) perpetually surrounded with myriads of worshippers who *see his face, and* like the high priest when clothed in his richest robes, *have his name* written *in their foreheads:* (Rev. xxii. 4:) instead of the feeble rays of that golden candlestick, whose lamps shone in the holy place, the heavenly temple is illuminated in a more glorious manner, *and needs no candle, neither light of the sun, for the glory of God* continually *enlightens it, and the Lamb is the light thereof:* (Rev. xxi. 23, xxii. 5:) Nay, we are assured that its sacred *ministers are made kings* as well as *priests unto God;* (Rev. i. 6;) and accordingly being *clothed in white raiment,* they have *crowns of gold on their heads;* (Rev. iv. 4;) as well as *harps and golden vials,* or censers *full of incense in their hands:* (Rev. v. 8:) and lest we should think these pompous services are only the entertainments of some peculiarly sacred seasons, we are told that *they rest not day nor night,* (Rev. iv. 8,) adoring *him that sits upon the throne,* and are fixed as *pillars in* his *temple, to go out no more.* Rev. iii. 12. Again, if it be spoken of as a crown, it is represented as *incorruptible;* (1 Cor. ix. 25;) *a crown of glory that fadeth not away.* 1 Pet. v. 4. And when it is called a kingdom, the scripture does not only add, as here in the text, that it is *the kingdom of God*, which must certainly exalt the idea of it; but that it is *a kingdom which can not be moved*, (Heb. xii. 28,) an *everlasting kingdom:* (2 Pet. i. 11;) nay, to carry our thoughts to the highest degree of dignity and glory, it is spoken of as a *sitting down with Christ on his throne.* Rev. iii. 21.

But further, the value of these illustrious representations is much enhanced, if we consider the character of the persons by whom they are made. They were persons well acquainted with these things, having received their information from a Divine revelation, and from the immediate visions of God. They were also persons of such sublime and elevated sentiments, that they had a sovereign contempt for all the enjoyments of time and sense, even those which the generality of mankind set the greatest value upon: *and counted all things but loss for the knowledge of Christ,* (Phil. iii. 8,) *and the testimony of a good conscience,* (2 Cor. i. 12,) *while they looked not at temporal, but at eternal things.* 2 Cor. iv. 18. They could deliberately, constantly, and even cheerfully, resign all the riches and honors, and carnal pleasures, which they might have purchased by their apostacy from religion; and were ready to embrace bonds, imprisonments, or death itself, when it met them in the way of their duty. Now certainly a glory, with which such holy, wise and heroic persons were so passionately enamored, and which they describe with such pathos of language, and such ecstasy of delight, while they were trampling with so generous a disdain on everything which earth calls good and great, must deserve our very attentive regard. And this it yet more evidently will appear to do, if we consider,

2. It is the state and world, which God has prepared for the display of his glory, and the entertainment of the most favored of his creatures.

This argument seems to be hinted at, when it is said, as in the place I referred to before, *eye hath not seen, nor ear heard, neither hath entered into the heart of man, the things which God hath prepared for them that love him.* 1 Cor. ii. 9. God well knows the capacity of his creatures, and how much happiness they are able and fit to receive; and he can fill their capacities to the utmost: nay, he can farther enlarge them to what degree he pleases, that they may admit superior degrees of. glory and felicity. A happiness, therefore, which he has prepared on purpose to display the riches of his magnificence and love, and to show what he can do to delight his creatures, must certainly be in some measure proportionable, if I may so express it, to the infinity of his own sacred perfections. Let us then seriously consider who God is; and attentively dwell in our meditations on the extent of his power, and the riches of his bounty; and our conception of the happiness of heaven must be raised to something more glorious, than the most emphatical words can perfectly describe.

And here, to assist our imagination in some degree, let us look round us, and take a survey of this visible world. This earth, how conveniently has he furnished it, how beautifully has he disposed it, how richly has he adorned it! What various and abundant provision has he made for the subsistence, the accommodation, and the entertainment of the creatures that inhabit it! and especially of man, in whom this scheme and system of things appears to centre, and to whom it is almost wisely and graciously referred! Yet earth is the habitation of a race of mean and degenerate creatures, who are but in a state of trial; nay, it is the habitation of thousands and ten thousands of God's incorrigible enemies, with whom *he is angry every day.* Psa. vii. 11. Already it is marked with some awful characters of the Divine displeasure: and the scripture assures us, that it is *reserved unto fire, against the day of judgment, and perdition of ungodly men.* 2 Pet. iii. 7. Yet even this earth is not a spectacle unworthy our regard; nor can we, if we allow ourselves to survey it with becoming attention, behold it without an affecting mixture of admiration, of love, and of joy—passions that will strike us yet more powerfully, if from this earth of ours we raise our eyes to the visible heavens; and there behold the glory of the sun, the brightness of the moon, and all the numerous host of heaven that attend in her train. Who that considers, with any degree of attention, their magnitude, their lustre, their motion, and their influence, can forbear crying out, *Oh Lord, our Lord, how excellent is thy name in all the earth! who hast set thy glory above the heavens.* Psal. viii. 1.

And when, with even these in our view, we further reflect, that there is another apartment, as yet invisible, of which this spangled firmament is but, as it were, the shining vail; an apartment, where the great Creator and Governor of all has fixed his stated residence, and erected the throne of his glory; even that throne which is forever surrounded by all the most holy and excellent of his creatures; we must be convinced, it is something more beautiful, and more magnificent than this harmonious system itself. And, methinks, when we have said more beautiful and more magnificent than this, imagination is ready to fail us, and to leave the mind dazzled and overwhelmed with an effulgency of lustre which it cannot delineate, and can scarce sustain. Yet will our venerable apprehensions of it be farther assisted if we consider,

3. That the kingdom of heaven is the great purchase of the blood of God's only begotten Son; and therefore to be sure it must be inconceivably valuable.

If you are at all acquainted with your Bibles, you must know that we are by sin in a state of *alienation from God;* (Ephes. iv. 18;) that we had forfeited all our title to his love, and stood justly exposed to his severe displeasure; and that it is *Jesus who delivered us from the wrath to come.* 1 Thess. i. 10. Now if we owe it to his merit and atonement *that we live,* (1 John iv. 9,) much more are we to ascribe it to him, if we are raised to any superior degree of happiness. If God could not, with honor to his justice, have suffered us, without such a propitiation, to have passed off with impunity; much less could he, without it, have received us to his embraces, and have advanced us to *sit with him on his throne.* Rev. iii. 21. Accordingly it is said of the blessed martyrs in the heavenly world, even of those who had so gloriously distinguished their fidelity and zeal, and *loved not their lives unto the death;* (Rev. xii. 11,) that they had *washed their robes, and made them white in the blood of the Lamb;* (Rev. vii. 14;) and they gratefully acknowledge it in their hymns of praise, that *Christ had redeemed them to God by his blood, and had made them kings and priests unto God.* Rev. v. 9, 10.

Now let us seriously reflect, and consider what this blood of the Lamb is. The apostle Peter tells us, that *silver and gold,* and all the peculiar treasures of kings and princes, are but *corruptible things,* (1 Pet. i. 18, 19,) or perishing and worthless trifles, when compared with it. And no wonder it is represented in such exalted language, when we consider it was the blood of the only begotten Son of God, who is *the brightness of* his Father's *glory, and the express image of his person,* (Heb. i. 3,) and indeed *one with him,* (John x. 30,) being possessed of a nature truly and properly divine; so that it is called *the blood of God.* Acts xx. 28. We may well argue, even from these transient surveys, that it was some important happiness, which he came to procure at so expensive a rate. Had an angel been sent down from heaven, we should naturally have concluded, it must have been upon some momentous errand: surely then, when the Lord of angels comes down, not only to live on earth, but to expire in bitter agonies on the cross, to purchase a benefit for us, we may be well assured, that this benefit must be very considerable. Our Lord Jesus Christ must certainly set a very great value upon it, or he would not have purchased it at such a price; and we are sure, the value that he apprehended in it must be its true value. He could not be imposed upon by any false appearance of glory and splendor: he despised, with a just and generous contempt, *all the kingdoms of the world, and the glory of them;* (Matt. iv. 8, 10;) and he was also well acquainted with the celestial kingdom, having so long dwelt in it, and so long presided over it: yet so highly does he esteem it, that he speaks of it upon all occasions, as the highest possible gift of Divine bounty, the richest preparation and noblest contrivance of Divine love: yea, he regards it as a felicity so great, that when he conducts his people into it, with the last solemn pomp of the judgment day, it is said, *he shall see of the travail of his soul, and be satisfied,* (Isa. liv. 11,) allowing it to be a just equivalent for all he has done, and all he has suffered in so glorious a cause.

4. The excellency of the heavenly kingdom will further appear, if we consider, that it is the main work of the Spirit of God upon men's hearts, to prepare them for an admittance into it.

You well know, that the blessed Spirit of God

is spoken of as that Divine Agent, by whom *all the hosts of heaven were created*, and all God's various works produced; (Job xxxiii. 4;) and it is *he* that *knows the things of God* even as *the human spirit knows the things of a man.* 1 Cor. ii. 11. Now it is his peculiar office in the economy of our redemption, to form the soul to a meetness for glory. Accordingly, when the apostle Paul had been reminding the Corinthians, that while they continued in their sinful state, they were unfit for the kingdom of God, he adds, *But ye are washed, but ye are sanctified, but ye are justified, in the name of the Lord Jesus, and by the Spirit of our God.* 1 Cor. vi. 11.

That the Spirit should condescend to engage at all in such a work, must give us a very sublime idea of the end at which it aims. But much more will that idea be raised, when we consider with what a variety, and what a constancy of operations he begins, continues, and perfects it. He attempts it, as we shall hereafter more particularly show you, sometimes by convictions of terror, and sometimes by insinuations of love; and by one method or another, in the hearts of all the heirs of this glory, he works so great a change, that it is represented by *turning a heart of stone into a heart of flesh*, (Ezek. xxxvi. 26,) by *raising the dead from their graves*, (Ezek. xxxvii. 13. Eph.

ii. 5, 6,) yea, by *producing a new creation.* 2 Cor. v. 17. Eph. ii. 10. For this does he watch over the soul with the tenderest care, and continues his friendly offices, to recover it from relapses, and gradually to form it to advancing degrees of sanctity, till at length it be enabled to *perfect holiness in the fear of God.* 2 Cor. vii. 1. Nay, so intent is this Sacred Agent on the important work, that when sinners most insolently and ungratefully reject him, and by resisting him oppose their own happiness, he does not immediately leave them; he strikes them again and again; and waits upon them for succeeding days and months, and years.

And when, perhaps, *the sincere convert* makes the most ungrateful return for the experience of his goodness, even after he has acknowledged, and at length obeyed it: when under the fatal transport of some ungoverned passion, and the influence of some strong temptation, he acts as if he were intent upon tearing down the work of the Spirit of God upon his soul, and driving him forever away; yet in how many instances does he return again after all these injuries, pleading the cause of God with a sweetly prevailing eloquence, and thus healing the wound, and repairing the breach, and making it perhaps stronger than before! And all this, for what? That the happy subject of all these kind operations may be formed to a fitness for the kingdom of heaven.

And are we to regard this blessed Spirit as an unmeaning agent, or as incapable of judging of the importance of this end for which he acts? Is that almighty energy of his employed in an insignificant manner? Surely Nicodemus, slow of understanding as he was, must apprehend the *importance of entering into the kingdom of heaven,* when he heard, that in order to be admitted to it, *a man must be born of the Spirit.* And let me add once more,

5. That the excellency of the heavenly kingdom may further be argued from the eagerness with which the enemy of souls is endeavoring to prevent our entrance into it.

You know the devil is always represented as the inveterate enemy of our happiness. His rage is expressed by that of *a roaring lion, that walks about, seeking whom he may devour:* (1 Peter v. 9:) and with unwearied diligence he is continually employed in forming and pursuing his temptations. And this is the grand design of all, that he may exclude us from the promised felicity. While sinners are in their unregenerate state, he endeavors to engage all their regards to the objects of time and sense; and for that purpose he continually presents them with a variety of entertainments and amusements suited to their respective tempers and circumstances. If they are awakened to any serious concern about their eternal salvation, he uses his utmost address to divert their minds from an attendance to it: and for this purpose he displays before them all the allurements of sin in its most engaging forms, and if they are not captivated with these, he often puts on a face of terror, and endeavors to affright them from religion by the most gloomy representations of it, or by horrible and distracting suggestions, that it is now forever too late to attain it.

Or, if Divine Grace surmount all this opposition, and the sinner resolutely chooses his portion in heaven, and puts his soul into the hands of Christ to be conducted to it, the malice of Satan pursues him even to that sacred retreat, which he has sought in the arms of his Saviour: and if he cannot prevent the soul from entering into heaven, he will at least labor to bring it into such a state of negligence, and to seduce it into those delays and relapses, which may divert its regards to that blessed world, which may cloud its evidences of it, and may at least, as much as possible, diminish the degree of its glory there.

Now permit me, in this instance, to turn the artillery of this cunning enemy against himself, and to argue the excellency of this kingdom, from the zeal and attachment with which he endeavors to obstruct your attaining it. Though Satan be now a very degenerate creature, he was once an angel of light, and still retains much of the knowledge, though he has lost the rectitude and integrity of the angelic nature. And he particularly knows what heaven is because he was once an inhabitant there; and while he is endeavoring to persuade the sinner to prefer earth before it, he does, by that very endeavor, incontestably prove, that he himself knows the contrary, and is fully apprized that there is nothing here to be compared with the felicity of the future state. And therefore while he seeks the destruction of the soul, he can leave it in the enjoyment of all its worldly prosperity; nay, he will attempt to lead him into methods, by which this prosperity may be promoted and increased.

And thus, sirs, I have endeavored a little to represent to you, what this kindom of heaven is from which we are assured that unconverted sinners shall forever be excluded. I have argued its excellency—from the representations which are made of it in the word of God—from its being the preparation of Divine love—from its being the purchase of a Redeemer's blood—and the end to which, on the one hand, the glorious operations of the blessed Spirit lead—and of which, on the other hand, all the stratagems and assaults of the prince of darkness are intended to deprive us. If, therefore, there be truth in scripture, if there be wisdom in heaven, or policy in hell, it must surely be infinitely important. And will any of you be such mean-spirited creatures, as, when that happiness is proposed to you, basely to relinquish the pursuit of it, and to sacrifice this blessed hope to any perishing trifle of mortal life? Surely it would be madness; though nothing more were to be apprehended than the loss of it; and though, when heaven were lost, all that earth can give should remain, if not to counterbalance the loss, yet at least to make you less sensible of it. But the weight of the argument will much more evidently appear, if you consider,

Secondly, *What will at last become of all those* who are excluded from this heavenly kingdom?

And here I beseech you to ask your own consciences, whether they be not inwardly persuaded, that those who are excluded from heaven, will remain in a state of existence, in which they will be ever sensible of their loss, and will be delivered over by Divine vengeance into that seat of torment, which God has prepared for the punishment of his implacable and incorrigible enemies.

This many of you do undoubtedly believe of such persons in general; believe it, therefore, of yourselves, if you are, and continue, in an unregenerate state.

1. You will still continue in a state of existence, in which you will be ever sensible of your unspeakable loss.

It might afford some wretched kind of consolation to you, if, as soon as you died out of this world, your being or your apprehensive powers were immediately to cease. Then the loss of heaven would only be an affliction to you in your dying moments, when you saw the enjoyments of earth were come to an end, and that you must have no part in any future happiness. But, alas! sirs, you cannot but know that when your bodies are dead, and consumed in their graves, your thinking faculties will still be continued to you: and, oh, that you would seriously reflect, how they will then be employed! You will then be thinking what you have done in life, what you have chosen for your happiness, and what has been the consequence of that choice. You will look round in vain for such accommodations and pleasures as you were once most fond of: but they will be no more. And when you perceive them vanished, like the visionary amusements of a dream, you will lift up your astonished eyes towards the regions of glory. And you indeed will have a lively view of those happy regions: but to what purpose will that view serve? Only through the righteous vengeance of God to aggravate your misery and despair.

"Alas," you will think, "there are millions of creatures yonder in heaven, who are rejoicing in the sight and favor of God, and are as full of happiness as their natures can contain, and shall be so forever; while I am cut off from all share in the Divine bounty. Rivers of pleasures are flowing in upon them, while not one drop is sent down to me; nor could I obtain it, though I were to ask the favor from the least of Christ's servants there. I am cast out as an accursed wretch, with whom God and his holy and blessed creatures will have no farther intercourse, or communion. And why am I thus cast out? and why am I thus cut off from God's favor, and driven from his presence, while so many that dwell with me on earth are admitted to it? My nature was originally as capable of happiness as theirs: and though it was sadly degenerate, it might, like theirs, have been renewed. God was once offering me that grace, by which my disordered soul might have been transformed, and I might have been fitted for the regions of glory: but I despised all these offers, and gave the preference to those fading vanities, which, alas! have forever forsaken me. And now *they that were ready are gone in* to the delightful banquet, *and the door is shut;* (Matt. xxv. 10;) the everlasting gates are shut forever, and barred against me. And here I must lie at this miserable distance, envying and raging at their happiness—of which, whatever sight or knowledge I may have of it, I must never, never, never partake!"

Such reflections, as these, sirs, will cut deep into your souls; and accordingly our Lord declares to impenitent sinners in his own days, *There shall be weeping and gnashing of teeth, when you see* others *sitting down in the kingdom of God, and you yourselves thrust out.* Luke xiii. 28. And if you would reflect, you might easily apprehend this. How would you be enraged at yourselves, if by your folly you had neglected securing a plentiful estate, when it was offered to you on the most easy terms; and you actually saw others, once your equals, and perhaps your inferiors, in the possession of it, in consequence of having taken those methods which you stupidly neglected? The reflection, I doubt not, would very much impair the pleasure you might find in other comfortable and agreeable circumstances. How much more insupportable then will the loss of heaven appear to you, when you come to see, and know, what it is you have lost, and have nothing to relieve or support you, under the painful recollection ?

It is to no purpose to object, that upon the principles of my last discourse, there will be no room to lament your exclusion from those entertainments, which you would be incapable of relishing if you were admitted to them: for you will then see, and lament that incapacity as a very great misery. As if a man, who was naturally fond of feasting and mirth, should see a great many regaling themselves, and reveling about him, while he was languishing under some painful distemper, which made him incapable of joining in the entertainment; he would yet grieve that he had no part in it: and it would be the increase, rather than the alleviation of his uneasiness, that it was his sickness which unfitted him for it; especially if, as in your case, it was a sickness, which he had brought upon himself by his own folly, and for which he had been offered an easy, pleasant, and infallible remedy, which he had refused to use till the malady was grown utterly incurable. One would imagine, this thought would be enough to impress you; but if it do not, let me entreat, and even charge you, to consider.

2. That if you are excluded from the king-

dom of heaven, you will be consigned over to those regions of darkness, despair, and misery, which God has prepared for those unhappy criminals, who are the objects of his final displeasure, and whom he will render everlasting monuments of his wrath.

There is something in human nature, that starts back at the thought of annihilation with strong reluctance: and yet how many thousands are there in this miserable world, who would with all their souls fly to it as a refuge! *They shall seek death*, as an inspired writer strongly expresses it, *and shall not find it; and shall desire to die, and death shall flee from them.* Rev. ix. 6. I will not attempt to enter into a detail of the horrors, attending the place and state, into which all who are excluded from the glories of the heavenly world shall be cast, and in which they shall be fixed. Let that one awful scripture suffice for a specimen of many more; in which we are told, that *every one whose name was not found written in the book of life*, or who was not registered in the number of those, who were to inhabit the New Jerusalem, or the kingdom of heaven, *was cast into the lake of fire*, (Rev. xx. 25,) or, as it is afterwards expressed, *into the lake that burns with fire and brimstone.* Rev. xxi. 8. Think of this, and ask your own hearts, you that are so impatient of the little evils of mortal life, whether you can endure to take up your abode forever in devouring fire, or whether you can *dwell with everlasting burnings?* Isa. xxxiii. 14. Yet these are the images by which the word of God represents it; to be plunged as in a sea of liquid fire, whose flames are exasperated and heightened, by being fed with brimstone; nay, as the prophet speaks, by a copious stream of brimstone, so expressly appointed by God himself, that this, as well as *the river of the water of life*, is represented as *proceeding* immediately from him: *he has made Tophet deep and large: the pile thereof is fire and much wood, and the breath of the Lord, like a stream of brimstone, doth kindle it.* Isa. xxx. 33.

It is painful to a tender mind to think of this, as what its fellow-creatures are obnoxious to: it is grievous to speak of it in these dreadful terms. But who are we, that we should be more merciful than God? Or rather, how can we imagine it is mercy, to avoid speaking of the appointment of infinite wisdom, for the punishment of impenitent sinners? What mercy were that, sirs, to avoid to mention these terrors to you, and to neglect to warn you of them, because they are great? which is indeed the very reason why the scripture thus pathetically describes them.

Away therefore with this foolish, this treacherous compassion, which chooses rather to leave men to be consumed, than to disturb their slumbers. Think, sirs, of that wretched man, whom Christ describes as *lifting up his eyes in hell, being in torments; seeing* the regions of the blessed at an unapproachable distance, and *begging in vain* that *one drop of water* might be sent *to cool his tongue*, amidst all the raging thirst with which he was *tormented in this flame*. Luke xvi. 23, 24. Regard it attentively; for as God lives, and as your soul lives, if you continue in an unrenewed state, you see in that wretch the very image and representation of yourselves. Yes, sinners, I testify it to you this day, that intolerable as it seems, it will on that supposition be your own certain fate; or to speak much more properly, your righteous, but inevitable doom. Heaven and earth will desert you in that dreadful hour: or if the inhabitants of both were to join to intercede for you, it would be in vain. Sentence will be past, and execution done. Hell will open its mouth to receive you, and shut it again forever to enclose you, with thousands, and ten thousands more, among whom you will not find one to comfort you, but every one ready to afflict you. Then shall you know the value which God sets upon his heavenly kingdom, by the judgments he inflicts upon you for neglecting and despising it; and then shall you know the importance of being born again, that only means by which Hell can be avoided, and Heaven secured.

And let me farther add, that conviction will quickly come in this terrible way, if you are not now prevailed upon to consider these things; things which, if you have the least regard to the word of God, you cannot but notionally believe. Do not then go about to annihilate, as it were, these prospects to your mind, by placing them at a long distance. The distance is not so great as to deserve mention. The patience of God will not wait upon you for thousands, or even hundreds of years; you have a few mortal days, in which to consider of the matter; or rather, you have the present moment to consider of it. And if you improve the opportunity, it is well; but if not, the just and uniform methods of the divine administration shall proceed, though it should be to your ruin. God has vindicated the honors of his violated law, and despised Gospel, upon millions, who with the rebel-angels, by whom they have been seduced, are even now *reserved in everlasting chains under darkness, unto the judgment of the great day;* (Jude, verse 6;) and he will as surely vindicate them upon you. *If you do not repent,* if you are not regenerate, *you shall all likewise perish,* (Luke xiii. 3,) and not one of you shall escape.

And thus I close this copious and important argument: this argument, in which life and death, salvation and damnation are concerned. View it, my friends, in all its connection, and see in what part of it the chain can be broken. Will you say, that without regeneration you can secure an interest in the kingdom of heaven, though the constitution of heaven oppose it, and all the declarations of God's word stand directly against it; and though nature itself proclaim, and conscience testify your incapacity to enjoy it? Or will you say, that being excluded from it, you shall suffer no considerable damage, though you lose so glorious a state, the noblest preparation of Divine love, the purchase of redeeming blood, and the end of the Spirit's operation on the soul; though you ever remain sensible of your loss, and be consigned over to dwell in that flaming prison, which God has prepared for the devil and his angels, and where all the terrors of his righteous judgment are made known?

But if you are indeed inwardly convinced of the truth and importance of these things, and will go away, and act as before, without any regard to them, I can say no more The reason of man, and the word of God can point out no stronger arguments, than an infinite good on the one hand, and an infinite evil on the other.

Hear, therefore, *O heavens! and give ear O earth!* and let angels and devils join their astonishment; that creatures, who would strenuously contend, and warmly exert themselves, I will not say merely for an earthly kingdom, but in an affair where only a few pounds, or perhaps a few shillings or pence were concerned, are indifferent here, where, by their own confession, a happy or miserable eternity is in question. For indifferent, I fear, some of you are and will continue. I have represented these things in the integrity of my heart, as in the sight of God, not in artful forms of speech, but in the genuine language, which the strong emotions of my own soul, in the views of them, most naturally dictated. Yet I think it not at all improbable, that some of you, and some perhaps who do not now imagine it, will, as soon as you return home, divert your thoughts and discourses to other objects; and may, perhaps, as heretofore, lie down upon your beds without spending one quarter of an hour, or even one serious minute, in lamenting your miserable state before God, and seeking that help and deliverance which his grace alone can give. But if you thus lie down, make, if you can, *a cove-*

nant with death that it may not break in upon your slumbers ; *and* an *agreement with hell,* (Isa. xxviii. 15,) that before the return of the morning, it may not flash in upon your careless souls another kind of conviction, than they will now receive from the voice of reason and the word of God.

DISCOURSE VII.

OF THE NECESSITY OF DIVINE INFLUENCES TO PRODUCE REGENERATION IN THE SOUL.

TITUS III. 5, 6.

Not by works of righteousness, which we have done, but according to his mercy he saved us, by the washing of regeneration, and renewing of the Holy Ghost; which he shed on us abundantly, through Jesus Christ our Saviour.

IF my business were to explain and illustrate this scripture at large, it would yield an ample field for accurate criticism and useful discourse, and more especially would lead us into a variety of practical remarks, on which it would be pleasant to dilate in our meditations. It evidently implies that those, who are saved of the Lord, are brought to the practice of good works, without which *faith is dead,* (James ii. 17,) and all pretences to a saving change are not only vain, but insolent. Yet it plainly testifies to us, that our salvation, and acceptance with God, is not to be ascribed to these, but to the Divine mercy;

which mercy operates by sanctifying our hearts, through the renewing influence of the Holy Spirit: And that there is an abundant effusion of this Spirit under the Gospel, which is therefore, with great propriety, called *the ministration of the Spirit*, (2 Cor. iii. 8,) and the *law of the Spirit of life in Christ Jesus.* Rom. viii. 2.

But I must necessarily, in pursuance of my general scheme, waive several of these remarks, that I may leave myself room to insist on the grand topic I intend from the words.

I have already shown you, who may be said to be in an unregenerate state: I have also described the change which regeneration makes in the soul; and have largely shown you, in the three last discourses, the absolute necessity and importance of it. And now I proceed,

To show the NECESSITY OF THE DIVINE POWER, in order to produce this great and important change.

This is strongly implied in the words of the text: in which the apostle, speaking of the method God has been pleased to take for the display of his goodness in the salvation and happiness of fallen men, gives us this affecting view of it, that it is *not by works of righteousness which we*, i. e. any of us Christians, *have done; but according to his* free grace and *mercy* that *he* has *saved us by the washing of regeneration, and the renewing of the Holy Ghost.* . . . . .

Lest any should imagine, that an external ceremony (baptism) was sufficient, or that it was the chief thing intended, the apostle takes the matter higher. And as the apostle Peter tells us, that the *baptism* which *saves us* is *not* merely *the putting away the filth of the flesh, but the answer of a good conscience towards God;* (1 Pet. iii. 21;) so the apostle Paul here adds, that we are saved *by the renewing of the Holy Ghost:* by which I can by no means understand something entirely distinct from, and subsequent to his regenerating influences; for according to the view of regeneration stated in our former discourses, none can be regenerated who are not renewed: but it seems to explain the former clause, and to refer to the more positive effect produced by Divine grace on the soul, whereby Christians are not only purified from sin, but disposed to, and quickened in a course of holy obedience. And then he further tells us, that *this Spirit is the gift of God,* and is plentifully communicated to us in the name, and through the hands of the blessed Redeemer, *being shed on us abundantly by God, through Jesus Christ our Saviour.*

Agreeably therefore to the general design and

purport of these words, I shall go on to demonstrate the absolute necessity of a Divine agency and operation in this great work of our regeneration; which I shall do from a variety of topics. And here I shall studiously waive many controversies, with which the Christian world has been afflicted, and the soundest part of it disturbed, with relation to the kind and manner of this influence. I will not so much as mention them, and much less discuss them; *lest Satan should take an advantage of us*, (1 Cor. ii. 11,) to divert our minds from what is essential in this doctrine, to what is merely circumstantial. Only let it be observed in general, that I speak of such an agency of God on our minds, as offers no violence to the rational and active nature which God has given us, nor does by any means supersede our obligation to those duties which his word requires; but on the contrary, cures and perfects our nature, and disposes the soul to a regard to such incumbent duties, and strengthens it in the discharge of them. With this only preliminary, which appears to me highly important, I proceed to show the reasonableness of ascribing this change to a Divine agency, rather than to anything else, which may be supposed to have any share in producing it. And we may infer this,

First, from the general and necessary dependence of the whole created world upon God.

There was a philosophical as well as Divine truth, in that observation of the apostle Paul at Athens, which was well worthy the most learned assembly ; *In him*, i. e. *in God, we live, and move, and have our being.* Acts xvii. 28. Such is the innate weakness of created nature, that it continually depends on a Divine support. The very idea of its being created, supposes that it had no cause of its existence, but the Divine will in the first moment of it ; and if it could not then subsist without that will, in the first moment of its existence, it neither could subsist without it in the second, or in any future moment of it ; since to have been dependent for a while, can never be supposed to render anything for the future independent. The continued existence then of all the creatures—no less of angels, than of worms, or trees, or stones—does properly depend upon the Divine energy which bears them up ; and holds those of them in life, which live, and those of them in being, which are inanimate, or without life.

And if their being be dependent, then surely it will follow, that all their perceptive and active powers, whatsoever they are, must continually depend upon God : for to exist with such powers is evidently more than simply to exist; and if a Divine agency be necessary for the latter, much more must we allow it to be necessary for the former.

The human mind, therefore, with all its capacities and improvements, must acknowledge itself perpetually indebted to God, who is the fountain of truth and wisdom, as well as of being: accordingly we are told, it is *he that teacheth man knowledge*. Psal. xciv. 1. All the *skill of the husbandman*, in one passage of Scripture, (Isa. xxviii. 26,) and all the *wisdom of the artificer*, in another, (Exod. xxxvi. 1, 2,) is ascribed to his influence: and if the improvement of the sciences, and any other discovery, which renders human life in any degree more commodious and agreeable, is to be ascribed to the Divine illumination and influence, then surely it is from hence this art of living wisely and well must also be derived. All the views upon which good resolutions are formed, all the strong impressions upon the mind arising from these views, and all the steadiness and determination of spirit, which does not only form such purposes, but carries them into execution, are plainly the effect of the Divine agency on the mind; without which no secular affairs could be clearly understood, strenuously pursued, or successfully accomplished. And how peculiarly reasonable it is, to apply this remark to the point now in view, will appear by attending,

Secondly, to the greatness and excellency of this regenerating change, which speaks it aloud to be the Divine work.

I must, upon this occasion, desire you to recollect what I laid before you in several of the former discourses. Think of the new light that breaks in upon the understanding; of the new affections that are enkindled in the heart; of the new resolutions, by which the will is sweetly and powerfully, though most freely influenced; and think of the degree of vigor attending these resolutions, and introducing a series of new labors and pursuits; and surely you must confess, that *it is the finger of God;* especially when you consider, how beautiful and excellent, as well as how great the work is.

Do we acknowledge, that it was the voice of God that first *commanded the light to shine out of darkness*, and that it was worthy of a Divine agency to produce so beautiful a creature as the sun, to gild the whole face of our world, and to dress the different objects around us in such a varied and vivid assemblage of colors? And shall we not allow it to be much more worthy of him, to lighten up a benighted soul, and reduce its chaos into harmony and order? Was it worthy of God to form the first principles even of the vegetative life, in the lowest plant or herb, and to visit with refreshing influences of the rain and sun the earth wherein these seeds are sown? And is it not much more worthy of him to implant the seed of the divine life, and to nourish it from time to time by the influence of his Spirit? Did it suit the Divine wisdom and mercy to provide for sustaining our mortal lives, for healing our wounds, and recovering us from our diseases? And shall it not much more suit him, to act as the great Physician of souls, in restoring them to ease, to health and vigor?

They must be dead indeed to all sense of spiritual excellence, who do not see how much more illustriously God appears, when considered as the author of grace, than merely as the author of nature. For indeed all the works of nature, and all the instances of Divine interposition to maintain its order and harmony, will chiefly appear valuable and important, when considered in subserviency to the gracious design of recovering apostate man from the ruin of his degenerate state—without which it had been far better for him never to have known being, and never to have inhabited a world so liberally furnished with a variety of good. And, therefore, I would appeal to every Christian, whether he does not find a much more ardent gratitude glowing in his heart when he considers God as the author of the religious and divine, than merely of the animal or the rational life?

And permit me here to remark, that, agreeably to these reasonings, some of the pagan philosophers have said very serious and remarkable things concerning the reality and the need of Divine influences on the mind, for the production of virtue and piety there. Thus, Seneca, when he is speaking of a resemblance to the Deity in character, ascribes it to the influence of God upon the mind: "Are you surprised," says he, "that man should approach to the gods? It is God that comes to men; nay, which is yet more, he enters into them; for no mind becomes virtuous but by his assistance."* Simplicius, also, was so sensible of the necessity of such an influence, that he "prays to God, as the father and guide of reason, so to co-operate with us, as to purge us from all carnal and brutish affections, that we may be enabled to act according to the dictates of reason, and to attain to the true knowledge of himself."† And Maximus Tyrius argues, agreeably to what is said above, that "if skill in the professions and sciences is insinuated into men's minds, by a Divine influence, we can much less imagine, that a thing so much more excellent, as virtue is, can

* Senec. *Epistol.* LXXIII. † Simplic. in Epictet. *ad fin.*

be the work of any mortal art; for strange must be the notion that we have of God, to think that he is liberal and free in matters of less moment, and sparing in the greatest."* And in the same discourse he tells us, "that even the best disposed minds, as they are seated in the midst, between the highest virtue and extreme wickedness, need the assistance and the help of God, to incline and lead them to the better side."† I am sensible that all these philosophers, with many more who speak to the same purpose, living after Christ's time, may be said to have learned such language from Christians: and if they did so, I wish all who have since worn the name had been equally teachable. But some who appeared much earlier, speak much in the same manner,‡ as I might easily show

* Max. Tyr. Dissert. xxii. † Max. Tyr. *ibid.*

‡ It is here remarkable, that *Xenophon* represents *Cyrus*, with his dying breath, "as humbly ascribing it to a *Divine influence* on his mind, that he had been taught to acknowledge the care of Providence, and to bear his prosperity with a becoming moderation."—Xen. Cyropæd. *lib.* viii. *cap.* 7, § 1. And Socrates is introduced, by Plato, as declaring, "that wheresoever virtue comes, it is apparently the fruit of a *Divine dispensation.*"—Plat. Men. *ad. fin. p.* 428. And to this purpose Plato has observed, "that virtue is not to be taught but by *Divine assistance.*"—Epinom. *pag.* 1014. And elsewhere he declares, "that if any man escape the temptations of life, and behave himself as becomes a worthy member of society, as the laws of it are generally settled"—which, by the way, is

you, if it were not already more than time to observe,

Thirdly. That we may further argue the Divine agency in this blessed work, from the violent opposition over which it prevails in its rise and progress.

The awakened soul, when laboring towards God, and aspiring after further communications of his grace to form it for his service, may justly say with David, *Lord, how are they increased that trouble me? How many are they that rise up against me?* Ps. iii. 1. With how many threatening dangers are we continually surrounded! And what a numerous host of enemies are ready to oppose us! *The law of sin, that wars in our members,* (Rom. vii. 23,) and concerning whose forces it may well be said, *their name is Legion, for they are many:* the evil influence of a degenerate world, whose corrupt examples press like a torrent, and require the most vigorous efforts to bear up against them: and in confederacy with these, and at the head of all, the Prince of Darkness—whose counsels and efforts, with relation to this world of ours, do as it were centre in this one thing, to prevent men's regene-

something very far short of religion—"he has reason to own, that it is God that saves him."—De Repub. *lib.* vi. *pag.* 677. *edit. Franc. of* 1602.

ration; because it is by means of this, *that those are recovered out of the snare of the devil, who were before led captive by him at his will.* 2 Tim. ii. 26.

I persuade myself, that when I am speaking on this head, though some may imagine it to be mere empty harangue, and common place declamation, the experienced soul will attest the truth of what I say. It may be some of you, who, by what of these sermons you have already heard, have come under some serious convictions, and been awakened in good earnest to be thoughtful about being born again, have felt such a struggle in your own minds that you may say, you never knew before what the *flesh*, the *world*, and the *devil* were, nor could have imagined that their opposition to this work was so forcible and violent as you now find it. To reform the irregularities of the life is comparatively easy; but to root sin out of the soul, to consecrate the whole heart to God, and demolish those idols that have been set up, as it were, in the secret *chambers of imagery*, (Ezek. viii. 12,) is difficult indeed; all the corruptions of the heart in such a case are ready to exert themselves, and it is natural for the *lusts of the flesh* to unite against that which is set upon destroying them all; nor did you ever know before, that there was such a world of sin within you. With violence also does the *strong man armed* exert himself, when *his goods* are about to be *taken from him* by one *stronger than himself:* as our Lord, with an unerring propriety and wisdom, represents it; (Luke xi. 21, 22;) and indeed it seems as if through the violence of his malignity, and the righteous judgment of God, who, whenever he pleases, can *take the wise in his own craftiness,* (1 Cor. iii. 19,) that Satan sometimes overshoots his mark, and raises so sensible an opposition against the cause of God in the soul, that an argument might be drawn, even from that very opposition, to prove the truth and excellency of what he sets himself so directly against. And you have now perhaps experienced, too, more than you ever did before, the inveterate opposition of the *seed of the Serpent* to *that of the Woman:* you have found, that since you began to think of religion in good earnest, some have derided you, others it may be have reviled you, and enemies have sprung up *out of your own house:* (Matt. x. 36;) though the impressions you have felt tend to make you more amiable, more kind, and more useful, and therefore one would think should conciliate their friendship: but this is a memorable instance in which self-love seems to make, as it were, a sacrifice of itself to the hatred of God. Now, therefore, to accomplish such a mighty change in the midst of such opposition, must evidently speak a Divine interposition. And surely the Christian, when thus recovered and restored, has reason to declare, as Israel did, *if it had not been the Lord who was on our side when* these confederate enemies *rose up against us, then they had swallowed us up quick, when their wrath was kindled against us; then the waters had overwhelmed us, the stream had gone over our soul, then the proud waters had gone over our soul,* (Psal. cxxiv. 1—5,) and would have quenched and buried every spark that looked like Divine life, and have borne away every purpose of reformation and holiness. The remark will be further illustrated, if we consider,

Fourthly, By what feeble means this change is accomplished.

The apostle observes, that in his day *they had the treasure* of the gospel lodged *in earthen vessels, that the excellency of the power,* which rendered it successful, *might* appear to *be of God and not of man.* 2 Cor. iv. 7. And it is still in a great measurc apparent, that the same method is made use of from the same principle. *The weapons of our warfare are not carnal;* and if at any time they are *mighty* and effectual, it must be only *through God.* 2 Cor. x. 4. It is *not by* secular *might or power,* (Zech. iv. 6,) that this great work is accomplished: no, nor by the refinements of learning, or the charms of eloquence. These things indeed have their use; the understanding may sometimes be convinced by the one, and the affections moved by the other: yet where both these have been done, the work often drops short: and it may be the plainest addresses, from a weak and almost trembling tongue, shall perform that which the far superior talents of many have not been able to effect. A multitude of such instances has been found, and perhaps seldom in these latter ages more observable than in the compass of our own observation.

Now whenever this work is accomplished by the preaching of the gospel in a Christian country, there is generally some circumstance that shows it is a divine, and not a human work. It is not the novelty of the doctrine which strikes; for all the main truths, on which the conviction and impression turns, have been known even from early infancy. No miracles awaken the attention, no new doctrines astonish the mind; but what has a thousand times been heard, and as often neglected, breaks in upon the mind with an almost irresistible energy, and strikes it as if it never had been heard of before. They seem as Israel did, *when the Lord turned again their captivity*, to awake out of a *dream*, (Ps. cxxvi. 1,) and wonder at the influence that has awakened them. The *ministry of the word* may seem but *feeble*, when compared to such an event: and yet sometimes even less solemn methods than that shall be effectual. One single text of scripture occurring to the sight or thought, one serious hint dropped in conversation, shall strike the mind, and pierce it through with an energy that plainly shows, that from whatever feeble hand it might seem to come, it was shot out of the *quiver of God*, and intended by him that made the heart to reach it: since there is almost as much disproportion between the cause and the effect, as between *Moses lifting up his rod* and the *dividing* of the water *of the sea* before Israel. Exod. xiv. 16. In many instances, remarkable providences, which one would have thought should have struck the soul as it were to the centre, have produced no effect: and yet a word, or a thought, has accomplished it; and after the *whirlwind*, the *earthquake*, and the *fire* have made their successive efforts in vain, it has appeared that *the Lord has been in the still small voice.* 1 Kings xix. 11, 12. On the whole, a variety of circumstances may illustrate the matter in different degrees; but, taking it in a general view, the remark appears to be well founded, that the weakness of the means, by which the saving change is wrought, argues plainly that the hand of God is in it: as when *anointing the eyes with spittle* gave *sight to the blind*, (John ix. 6,) it was evidently the exertion of a miraculous power. But now, agreeably to what has been advanced under these several heads, I shall proceed to show at large,

Fifthly, That the Scripture teaches us to ascribe this great change on the mind to a DIVINE AGENCY AND OPERATION.

And here you will see, that it does not merely drop here and there an expression which is capable of such an interpretation, but that the whole tenor of the word of God leads to such a conclusion: and surely, if we own the word to be divine, we need no more convincing argument of the truth of this remark. The only difficulty I shall here find, will be like that which occurred under the former head, and proceeds from the variety and multiplicity of texts which offer themselves to me while reflecting on this subject; however, I will endeavor to rank them in the plainest and best order I can, under the following particulars. We find God sometimes *promises* to produce such a change in men's minds; and at other times he *speaks* of it *as his own work*, when it has been already produced: the scripture represents even the *increase of piety* in a regenerate heart, as the effect of a Divine power; and how much more must the *first implanting* of it be so: nay, it goes yet further than this, and expresses *the necessity* as well as the *reality* of a Divine influence on the mind to make it truly religious, and resolves *the want of true religion* into this, that God withholds his influence. If, therefore, any one, and much more if all these particulars can be made out, I think it must force a conviction on your judgment at least, that what we are endeavoring to confirm in this discourse is the doctrine of scripture.

1. There are various places in scripture, wherein God *promises* to produce such a change in men's minds as we have before described; which plainly shows that it is to be acknowledged as his work.

Thus Moses says to Israel, without all doubt by the Divine direction, *The Lord thy God will circumcise thy heart, and the heart of thy seed, to love the Lord thy God with all thy heart, and with all thy soul, that thou mayest live.* Deut. xxx. 6. And this circumcision of the heart must surely be the removal of some insensibility and pollution adhering to it, and bringing it to a more orderly, regular, obedient state. It is sometimes made matter of *exhortation,* and thus indeed proves that there is a view in which it may be considered as a DUTY incumbent upon us (as when Moses said, *circumcise the foreskin of your heart;* (Deut. x. 16;) and Jeremiah, in imitation of him, *circumcise yourselves to the Lord, and take away the foreskin of your heart.* (Jer. iv. 4.) Here it is put in the form of a *promise*, to signify that wherever it was done, it was in consequence of God's preventing and assisting grace.

On the same principle, the Father promises to Christ, *thy people shall be willing in the day of thy power.* Ps. cx. 3. But if any pretend that these words may possibly admit of another version, though I know none more just than this, there are many other parallel places which are not attended with any ambiguity at all. Such, in particular, is that gracious promise, which though it was immediately made to the house of Israel, is nevertheless quoted by the apostles as expressive of God's gospel covenant with all believers; *After those days, saith the Lord, I will put my law in their inward parts, and write it in their hearts, and I will be their God, and they shall be my people:* (Jer. xxxi. 33; Heb. viii. 19:) or, as it is elsewhere expressed by the same prophet Jeremiah, *I will give them one heart and one way, that they may fear me forever; and I will put my fear in their hearts, that they shall not depart from me.* Jer. xxxiii. 32, 39, 40. And Ezekiel echoes back the same language by the same Spirit;

I will give them one heart, and I will put a new spirit within you; and I will take the stony heart out of their flesh, and will give them a heart of flesh; that they may walk in my statutes, and keep mine ordinances and do them; (Ezek. xi. 19, 20:) which is afterwards repeated again almost in the same words: *A new heart also will I give you, and a new spirit will I put within you: and I will take away the stony heart out of your flesh, and I will give you a heart of flesh; and I will put my Spirit within you, and cause you to walk in my statutes, and ye shall keep my judgments, and do them.* Ezek. xxxvi. 26, 27.

Now such a transformation of the heart and spirit as may be represented by a thorough renovation, or by changing stone into flesh, speaks the doctrine I am asserting in as plain terms as we could contrive or express; and beautifully points out at once the greatness and excellency of the change, and the Almighty power by which it is effected; for we may assure ourselves God would never promise such influences, if he did not really mean to impart them. But again,

2. Agreeably to the tenor of these promises, the scripture also *ascribes* this work to a Divine agency, when it is effected.

Thus the apostle John, when he is speaking of those who, on *receiving Christ, become the sons of*

God, declares concerning them that *they were born, not of blood, nor of the will of the flesh, nor of the will of man, but of God:* (John i. 13:) plainly intimating that it was to him, and not only or chiefly to themselves or others, that this happy change was to be ascribed: which is well explained by those words of St. James, in which he says, *of his own will begat he us with the word of truth, that we should be a kind of first-fruits of his creatures.* Jam. i. 18. Accordingly our Lord, as you have heard at large, insists upon it as absolutely necessary to a man's *entering into the kingdom of God,* not only that he should be born again, but more particularly that he should *be born of the Spirit,* (John iii. 3, 5,) i. e. by the sanctifying influence of the Spirit of God operating upon his soul, to purify and cleanse it.

And as this great work of regeneration chiefly consists in being brought to faith and repentance, you may observe, that each of these are spoken of as a Divine production in the mind, or as the gift of God to it. Thus the believing Jews, with one consent, expressed their conviction when they heard the story of Cornelius and declare, *then has God also to the Gentiles granted repentance unto life.* Acts xi. 18. And so the apostle Paul expresses it, when speaking of the possibility that some might be *recovered out of the snare of the devil,* he says, *If God peradventure will give them repentance to the acknowledging of the truth.* 2 Tim. ii. 25, 26. That very attention to the Gospel, which is the first step towards the production of faith in the soul, is resolved into this, when it is said, that *the Lord opened Lydia's heart, that she attended to the things which were spoken by Paul.* Acts xvi. 41. And with regard to the progress of it, it is not only said in general, *you hath he quickened, who were dead in trespasses and sins;* but *faith* is expressly declared to be *the gift of God;* (Eph. ii. 1, 8;) and the apostle says to the Philippians, that it was *given to them to believe;* (Phil. i. 29;) nay, it is represented as a most glorious and illustrious effort of Divine power, and ascribed to *the exceeding greatness of his power towards them that believe, according to the working of his mighty power which he wrought in Christ, when he raised him from the dead.* Eph. i. 19, 20.

And in this view it is, that this change is called *a new creation;* (2 Cor. v. 17;) plainly implying, as a celebrated writer well expresses it, "that something must here be done in us, and for us, which cannot be done by us." Wherefore it is said, that *the new man is renewed in knowledge after the image of him that created him:* (Col. iii. 10:) and *we are his workmanship, created in Christ Jesus unto good works:* (Eph. ii. 10:) not to insist upon the great variety of parallel passages, in which the same thoughts are expressed almost in the very same words. But he indeed who would reckon up all the scriptures, both in the Old and New Testaments, which directly or indirectly refer to this, must transcribe a larger part of both than would be convenient to read at one time in a worshiping assembly. But we may further, by a very strong consequence, infer the doctrine I am now maintaining from those various passages of the sacred writers, in which,

3. The *increase* of piety in a heart already regenerated, is spoken of as the work of God.

Thus David, even when he felt himself disposed to the most vigorous prosecution of religion, solemnly declares his dependence upon continued Divine influences, to enable him to execute the holy purpose he was then most affectionately forming: *I will run the way of thy commandments,* says he, *when thou shalt enlarge my heart,* (Psal. cxix. 32,) i. e. when thou shalt influence it with a steady principle of zeal, and with those devout passions which may make every branch of my duty easy and delightful. And the apostle Paul declares his persuasion that God would continue those gracious influences which he had already imparted: *He that has begun a good work in you, will perform it until the day of Jesus Christ.*

Phil. i. 6. And when he speaks of the ardent desire with which Christians were aspiring towards a better world, he adds, *He that hath wrought us for the self-same things is God.* 2 Cor. v. 5. Thus also he ascribes his continued fidelity in the ministry to the grace of God that was with him, as being *one that had obtained mercy of the Lord to be faithful:* (1 Cor. vii. 25 :) for *by the grace of God,* says he, *I am what I am:* and if *I have labored more abundantly than* others, it is *not I, but the grace of God which was with me.* 1 Cor. xv. 10. On the same principle he acknowledges, that the success of Apollos in watering, as well as his own in planting, was to be referred to this, that *God gave the increase* in the one case as well as in the other. 1 Cor. iii. 6, 7. And he concludes his Epistle to the Hebrews with this remarkable prayer: *The God of peace make you perfect in every good work to do his will, working in you that which is well-pleasing in his sight, through Jesus Christ.* Heb. iii. 31. But indeed, as every prayer that the apostles offer for any of their Christian brethren and friends, that they may *grow in grace,* might be urged for the illustration of this head, I choose rather to refer the rest to your own observation on this general hint, than to enter into a more particular enumeration. I shall only add, to complete the argument,

4. That the scripture often declares the *necessity* as well as the *reality* of such influences, and refers the ruin of man to this circumstance, that God in his righteous judgment had withheld or withdrawn them.

When Moses would upbraid the obstinacy of the Israelites, that all the profusion of wonders wrought for them in Egypt, and in the wilderness, had not produced any suitable impressions; so much was he accustomed to think of every thing good, in the moral, as well as in the natural world, as the gift of God, that he uses this remarkable expression: *Yet the Lord hath not given you a heart to perceive, and eyes to see, and ears to hear, unto this day.* Deut. xxix. 4. And our Lord, the propriety of whose expressions surely none can arraign, speaks to the same purpose, when adoring the Divine conduct with respect to the dispensation of saving light and gospel blessings, he says, *I thank thee, O Father, Lord of heaven and earth, that thou hast hid these things from the wise and prudent, and hast revealed them unto babes; even so, Father, for so it seemed good in thy sight.* Matt. xi. 25, 26. If some of the plainest and lowest of the people, who were in comparison to others but as little children, understood and received the gospel, while the learned men and politicians of the age despised it, God revealed it to the former, while he suffered the vail of prejudice to remain on the mind of the latter, though his Almighty hand could easily have removed it.

Those other words of our Lord must not be omitted here, in which he says, *No man can come unto me, except the Father which hath sent me draw him:* (1 John vi. 44 :) and what this *drawing of the Father* means, he himself has explained by saying, *No man can come unto me, except it be given him of my Father;* (Ver. 65 ;) and elsewhere he expresses it by *learning of the Father;* (Ver. 45 ;) all which must undoubtedly signify a Divine agency and influence on the mind. Nay, a more forcible expression than this is made use of by the evangelist John, where he takes notice of the unbelief of those that saw the miracles of Christ, *therefore they could not believe, because Esaias said, he has blinded their eyes, and hardened their hearts:* (John xii. 39, 40 :) which is agreeable to that expression of the apostle Paul, *he has mercy on whom he will have mercy, and whom he will he hardeneth:* (Rom. ix. 18 :) a thought which the apostle pursues at large through the following verses.

These, to be sure, are very emphatical scriptures: and though it is necessary to understand them in such a qualified sense as to make them consistent with other scriptures which charge men's destruction, not on any necessitating decree of God, but upon themselves and the abuse of their own faculties; yet still these expressions must stand for something; and in the most moderate sense that he can put upon them, they directly confirm what I have here brought them to prove. So that on the whole, the matter must come to this—That the cause of men's final and everlasting ruin may be referred in one view of it, to God's withholding those gracious influences, which if they had been imparted, would indeed have subdued the greatest perverseness; but his withholding these influences is not merely an arbitrary act, but the just punishment of men's wickedness; and of their obstinate folly in trifling with the means of his grace, and grieving his Spirit till he was provoked to withdraw. This thought, which I might largely prove to you to be a compendium of the scripture scheme, reconciles all; and any consequences drawn from one part of that scheme to the denial of the other, how plausible soever, must certainly be false.

I hope what I have here said may be sufficient to fix a conviction in your judgments and consciences, that regeneration is ultimately to be referred to a Divine influence upon the soul: or, as the apostle expresses it in the text, that *God saves us of his mercy, by the washing of regeneration, and renewing of the Holy Ghost, which he shed on us abundantly through Jesus Christ our Saviour.*

I shall conclude with two or three reflections, which, though so exceeding obvious, I shall touch upon, in regard to their great importance, without offering, as I might, to dilate on each of them at large.

1. Let those who have experienced this divine change in their souls give God the glory of it.

Perhaps there are many of you who may see peculiar reason to do it; perhaps you may be conscious to yourselves, that the arm of the Lord was remarkably revealed in conquering every sensible opposition, and getting itself the victory, even when you seemed, as if you had been resolutely bent upon your own destruction, to struggle to the utmost against the operation of his grace on your soul. Others may perhaps have perceived the strength of the Divine agency in the slightness of the occasion, or in the weakness of the means by which he wrought; which indeed is often matter of astonishment to those that seriously reflect upon it. But whatever your inclinations may have appeared, and whatever means or instruments were used, give God the glory of all.

If you have found yourselves, from your early years, inclined to attend to divine things, and susceptible of tender impressions from them, that attention and those impressions were to be resolved into this; that God prevented you with the blessings of his goodness. If you have enjoyed the most excellent public ordinances, even with all the concurrent advantages that the most pressing exhortations, and the most edifying example of parents, ministers, and companions could give; it was Divine Providence that furnished you with those advantages, and Divine grace that added efficacy to them—else they had only served to display their own weakness, even where they might have appeared most powerful, and to illustrate that insensibility or obstinacy of heart which would have rendered you proof against all. You do well indeed to honor those whom God has blessed as the means of your spiritual edification: but if they think aright, it would grieve them to the very heart to have those applauses given, and those acknowledgments made to them, which are due to God alone. All they have done is so little that it deserves not the mention; and the greater attainments they have made in religion, the more cordially will they join with the holy apostle in saying, *Neither is he that planteth anything, neither he that watereth, but God that giveth the increase.* 1 Cor. iii. 7.

2. We may further infer, that they who attempt the conversion of sinners, should do it with an humble dependence on the co-operation of Divine grace.

Otherwise they will probably find themselves fatally disappointed; and after their most skillful or most laborious attempts, they will complain that they *have labored in vain, and spent their strength for nought;* (Isa. xlix. 4;) and find reason to say, *The bellows are burnt, and the lead is consumed of the fire*, yet the dross is not *taken away*. Jer. vi. 29. A dependence upon God, in all the common affairs of life, becomes us as we are *creatures;* and it is most necessary that we should, *in all our ways acknowledge him*, as we expect or desire that *he should direct* or prosper *our paths:* (Prov. iii. 6:) but the greater the undertaking is, the more solemn should the acknowledgment of God be.

Let me therefore especially recommend this to those who are coming forth as young officers in the army of Christ. See to it, my brethren, that *in the name of your God you set up your banners;* (Psal. xx. 5;) that you apply from time to time to your public work with a deep conviction upon

21

your minds that no strength of reason will effectually convince, that no eloquence will effectually persuade, unless he that made men's hearts will plead his own cause, and bow those hearts in humble subjection. With these views, I have often known the feeblest attempts successful, and the meek and lowly have *out of weakness been made strong;* (Heb. xi. 34;) while for want of this, all the charms of composition and delivery have been at best but like *the lovely song of one who has a pleasant voice*, or the art of *one that can play well on an instrument.* Ezek. xxxiii. 32. It is *those that honor God* by the most cordial dependence upon him that *he delighteth to honor:* (1 Sam. ii. 30:) and I will presume to say, that it is the inward conviction of this important truth, which I feel upon my soul while I am confirming it to you, that encourages me to hope, *that this labor shall not be in vain in the Lord,* (1 Cor. xv. 58,) but that a Divine blessing shall evidently attend what has already been delivered, and what shall further be spoken. Only let me conclude my present Discourse with this one necessary caution,

3. That you do not abuse this doctrine of the *necessity of Divine influences,* which from the word of God, has been so abundantly confirmed.

God does indeed act upon us, in order to produce this happy change: but he acts upon us in a manner suitable to our rational nature, and not as if we were mere machines. He saves us, as the scripture expresses it, by awaking *us* to *save ourselves:* (Acts ii. 40:) *a new heart does he give us, and a new spirit does he put within us,* (Ezek. xxxvi. 26,) to stir us up to be solicitous *to make ourselves a new heart and a new spirit:* (Ezek. xviii. 31:) he *circumcises our heart to love him,* (Deut. xxx. 6,) by engaging *us* to *take away the foreskin of our hearts.* Jer. iv. 4. You see the correspondency of the phrases, and it is of great importance that you attend to it. If any therefore say, "I will sit still, and attempt nothing for my own recovery, till God irresistibly compels me to it:" he seems as like to perish, as that man would be, who, seeing the house in flames about him, should not attempt to make his escape, till he felt himself moved by a miracle.

Sirs, the dependence of the creature on God, though it be especially, yet it is not only, in spiritual affairs: it runs through all our interests and concerns. We as really depend upon his influence to stretch out our hands, as we do to raise our hearts towards him in prayer. Your fields could no more produce their fruit without his agency, than his word could, without it, become fruitful in your hearts: yet you plow and sow; and would look upon him as a madman, that upon this principle should decline it, urging, that no crop could be expected if God did not produce it; and that if he pleased to produce it, it would come up without any human labor. The argument is just the same in that case, as when men plead for the neglect of means or endeavors, from the reality and necessity of a divine concurrence. And if they apply this argument to the concerns of their souls, when they do not apply it to those of their bodies, it plainly shows, that they regard their bodies more than their souls; and that in pretending to make these excuses, they belie their conscience, and act against the secret conviction of their own heart. Such persons do not deserve to be disputed with, but rather should be solemnly admonished of the danger of such egregious trifling, where eternity is at stake.

And sure I am, that it is offering a great affront to the memory of the blessed Paul, when men pretend to encourage themselves in this perverse temper from anything he has said. For when he gives us, as it were, the substance of all I have now been saying, in those comprehensive words, *It is God that worketh in you, both to will and to do, of his good pleasure*, (Phil. ii. 13,) he is so far from mentioning it as an excuse for remissness and sloth, that he introduces it professedly in the very contrary view, as engaging us to exert ourselves with the utmost vigor in a dependence upon that Divine operation. And therefore, as he there expresses it, I say with him, *Work out your own salvation with fear and trembling;* and if you will not do it, you have reason to tremble in the prospect of a final condemnation from God, aggravated by your having thus irrationally and ungratefully abused the revelation of his grace.

DISCOURSE VIII

OF THE VARIOUS METHODS OF THE DIVINE OPERATION IN THE PRODUCTION OF THIS SAVING CHANGE.

1 Cor. xii. 6.

There are diversities of operations, but it is the same God which worketh all in all.

Whatever the original sense of these words was, and how peculiarly soever they may relate to the miraculous gifts of the Holy Spirit, the whole tenor of this discourse will show with how much propriety they may, at least, be accommodated to the operations of his grace. I have proved to you in the last of these lectures, that wherever regeneration is produced, it is ultimately to be ascribed to a Divine agency; and though I cannot say it is equally important, yet I apprehend it may be both agreeable and useful to proceed,

Fifthly, To survey the variety of methods which God is pleased to take in producing this happy change: or, to borrow the language of the text, to consider the *diversity of operations*, by which *the same God, who worketh all in all*, i. e. who produces all the virtues and graces of the Christian character, in some degree, in all his people, is pleased, according to his own wise and gracious purposes, to proceed in his agency, on those whom he regenerates and saves.

And this survey will not be matter of mere curiosity, but may probably revive the hearts of some amongst you by the recollection of your own experience: and it may be a caution to others, who, for want of due compass and extent of thought and knowledge, are ready to argue, as if God had but one way to work on the human heart, and that one the particular manner by which he recovered them. Of this I shall speak more largely hereafter. In the mean time, I judged it necessary to premise this hint, to direct us as to the temper with which this discourse should be heard, as well as to the purpose to which it is to be improved.

Now what I have to offer on this subject will be ranged under these three heads. There is a diversity and variety observable—in the *time*—the *occasion*—and the *manner*, of the Divine operations on the soul.

I. There is an observable variety, as to the TIME of God's gracious operations on different persons.

Some are called in their infancy:—others, and these perhaps the greatest part, are wrought upon in youth:—and some very few in the advance, and even in the decline of life.

1. Some are wrought upon by Divine grace in their *infancy.*

This is often the case; and I doubt not, but if parents were to do their duty, it would much more frequently be so. And it is an honor which God is pleased, in some instances, remarkably to confer on a good education; which is indeed so important a duty on one side, and so great a privilege on the other, that it is the less to be wondered at, that he so mercifully encourages Christian parents in the discharge of it: thus granting, as it were, an immediate *reward* for this *labor of love.* And I must here take the freedom, on my own observation, to say, that God seems especially to own the faithful endeavors of pious mothers in this respect. He has wisely and graciously given that sex a peculiar tenderness of address, and an easy and insinuating manner, which is admirably adapted to this great end, for which, no doubt, he especially intended it, that of conveying knowledge to children, and making tender impressions on their minds: and there is hardly any view in which the importance of the sex more evidently appears.

We have encouragement to believe, there are a considerable number who are, as it were, *sanctified from the womb,* and in whom the seeds of Divine grace are sown, before they grow up to a capacity of understanding the public preaching of the word: a remark, which Mr. Baxter carries so far as to say, that he believes, "if the duties of religious education were conscientiously discharged, preaching would not be God's ordinary method of converting souls: but the greater part would be wrought upon before they were capable of entering into the design of a sermon." And indeed it seems to me, that children may early come to have some apprehensions of what is most important in religion. They may have a reverence for God, and a love for him, as that great Father who made them, and that kind Friend who gives them everything that they have: they may have a fear of doing anything that would displease him; and though it is not so easy for them to understand the doctrines peculiar to a Redeemer, yet when they hear of Christ as the Son of God, who came down from heaven to teach men and children the way thither; who loved them, and did them good every day, and at last died to deliver them from death and hell; their little hearts may well be impressed with such thoughts as these, and they may find a growing desire *to be instructed* in what Christ is, and what he taught and did, and *to do* what shall appear to be *his will.* And wherever this is the prevailing disposition, it seems to me that the seeds of holiness are sown in that soul, though but small proficiency may be made in knowledge, and though the capacities for service be very low.

I will add, that some remarkably pertinent and solid things, which little children have said concerning religion, seem to me plainly to evidence, that they have been, in many instances, under some uncommon teachings of the Divine Spirit: and it seems perfectly suitable to the genius of Christianity, that in this sense God should *ordain strength out of the mouth of babes and sucklings,* (Psal. viii. 2,) and should *reveal* to them *what he has* suffered to be *hidden from the wise and prudent.* (Matt. xi. 25.) Nor can I suppose it hard for any, who have been for a considerable time acquainted with the state of religion in Christian societies, to recollect various instances, in which persons thus *taught of God,* who have heard, and known, and loved the scriptures, and delighted in ordinances and serious discourse from their childhood, have been, in some measure, like Samuel, Obadiah, Jeremiah, Josiah, and Timothy, honored with eminent usefulness in the church, and have happily filled some of its most important stations of service. Almost every age has afforded instances of this; and I am persuaded, many are now growing up amongst us, who will be instances of it in ages yet to come.

2. Others, and these perhaps the greatest part of real Christians, are wrought upon in their *youthful days.*

Many parents are very deficient in a due care to cultivate the infant minds of their little ones; or the feeble and general impressions then made are, perhaps, worn out and lost, in the growing vanities of childhood and youth. They begin to be drawn away by evil inclinations and examples, and by the delusions of a flattering world, which then puts on its most attractive charms, to gain upon their inexperienced minds: and hereupon they *follow after vanity, and become vain:* (2 Kings xvii. 15:) *of the rock which begat them, they* grow *unmindful, and forget the God that formed them.* Deut. xxxii. 18. But by one method or another, God often stops them in this dangerous career; and awakening ordinances, or more awakening providences, bring them to a stand, and turn them the contrary way. *The terrors of the Lord set themselves in array* against them; (Job. vi. 4;) or his mercy melts their souls, and they yield themselves its willing captives. They consecrate their hearts, warm as they are with youthful vigor, to be the sacrifices of Divine love, and enter, it may be, very early into the bonds of God's covenant: and so prove such *a seed to serve him*, as is *accounted to the Lord for a* most honorable and useful *generation.* Psal. xxii. 30. Blessed be God, I speak to many who know this by experience! By far the greater part of those who have been admitted to your communion, since I settled among you, have been, as I apprehend, under the age of twenty-four years: and several of those, who were farther advanced in life when they first approached the table of the Lord, had been brought to real religion in their much earlier years; though particular circumstances, or some mistaken apprehensions, might prevent their giving up their names publicly to the Lord, so soon as they might, and as they ought to have done it.

3. Some few are wrought upon by Divine grace in the *advance*, and even in the *decline* of life.

I confess that the number of these is comparatively small: and it is not to be wondered at, that it is so. They are not many who arrive at what can properly be called old age; and of them but a very inconsiderable part are then brought to anything which looks like a saving change. Nor shall we be much surprised at this, if we consider the inveterate nature of bad habits, which render it almost as hard for them *that are accustomed to do evil*, to *learn to do good*, as it is for *the Ethiopian to change his skin, or the leopard his spots.* Jer. xiii. 23. To such a degree are prejudices riveted in the mind, so insensible is it rendered of tender and generous impressions, so cold are the affections, and the habits, if the phrase may be allowed, so rigid, that, humanly speaking, there is much less probability of their being impressed with religion, than there was when they were in the bloom of life; notwithstanding all the seeming advantages which might arise from riper reason, deeper experience, and a nearer prospect of eternity. In all these things, it is in vain to reason against observation of fact, since we evidently see how uncommon a thing it is, for persons to be awakened and reformed in old age; especially if they have been educated in the principles of religion, and have made a florid profession of it in their youth—from which they have afterwards apostatized, out of a love to the wealth or honors of the world, or a relish for sensual delights. Such persons generally live and die monuments of Divine wrath, bearing, as it were, in characters dreadfully legible, the sad inscription of those, who having forsaken God, are finally forsaken of him. They appear as *dry trees, twice dead,* and fit for nothing but to be *plucked up by the roots, and cast into the fire.* Jude ver. 12; John xv. 16.

Nevertheless, to prove the infinite energy and sovereignty of Divine grace, God is sometimes pleased to work even on such. He touches the rock which has stood for ages unmoved, and the waters flow forth: he says to the dry bones, *Live,* and they obey; they are clothed with beauty, they are animated with life, and stand up as with the vigor of a renewed youth, to pursue the labors of religion, and to fight the *battles of the Lord.* Ezek. xxxviii. 20. Such instances, in which aged sinners have been thus wrought upon, I have read and heard; though, I grieve to say it, I can recollect very few, if any, that have occurred to me within the sphere of my own personal observation and acquaintance.

But besides this variety in the time, there is also,

II. An observable diversity, in the OCCASION, which Divine grace takes to operate upon different persons.

The occasions are indeed so various, that it would be impossible to enumerate them; I shall however just touch on some of the chief.

And here I might particularly consider a religious education in this view, and that daily converse with pious friends, which is of course connected with it. But though perhaps there may be no occasion more considerable in itself, and none that has been more eminently honored of God; yet it is proper to waive it here, as having been mentioned under the former head.

I proceed therefore further to observe, that some are wrought upon by the word of God; others by some remarkable providences; some by little incidents, which, inconsiderable as they seem in themselves, grow memorable by the noble effects they are made to produce: and others by secret and immediate impressions of God upon their spirits, which cannot be resolved into any external cause, or any visible occasion at all.

1. The administration of Divine ordinances, and especially the word of God and prayer, is an occasion, which he most frequently takes to work upon men's hearts by his grace.

I do not mention the administration of the sacraments upon this occasion; because, though they have so noble and effectual a tendency to improve men's minds in piety, and to promote Christian edification; yet I do not remember to have heard of any instance, in which they have been the means of men's conversion; which is the less to be wondered at, as they were appointed for a very different end.

There are many, however, that have been

wrought upon in prayer, as there are many things concur in this to awaken and impress the mind. The solemn acknowledgments then made of the Divine perfections, the praises offered to his tremendous Majesty, the deep and humble confession of our various and aggravated guilt in his holy presence, the lamentations over it, the importunate pleadings for a variety of blessings both for time and eternity; in a word, all the overflowings of pious affections in the breast of him that leads the devotion, and especially the earnest entreaties then offered for unconverted sinners, the genuine expressions of an undissembled apprehension of their danger, and the fervent breathings after Divine grace, to be communicated to them for their spiritual life: all these things, I say, and many more, which occur in prayer, when it is managed aright, may, by the Divine blessing, be singularly useful. And I am well assured, there have been happy instances, in which, *while* God's people *have yet been speaking* to him on this head, he has graciously *heard,* and signally *answered them.* Isa. lxv. 24.

But the reading, and especially the preaching of the word of God, is the grand occasion and instrument in the conversion of souls. *Of his own will he begets them with the word of truth:* (Jam. i. 18:) and it is admirably suited to those saving impressions which it is intended to make on the heart, *being quick and powerful, and sharper than any two-edged sword.* Heb. iv. 12. It was *while Paul was preaching* that *the Lord opened Lydia's heart, so that she attended to the things which were spoken* by him: (Acts xvi. 14:) and it was while Peter was thus employed, that such vast multitudes *were pricked in their hearts, and said to* him, *and to the rest of the apostles* present, *Men and brethren, what shall we do?* Acts ii. 37? And I am well persuaded, that various and lamentable as the instances are, in which men *stop their ears* and *harden their hearts* against it, God does not even to this day *leave it without witness:* but the *terrors of the Lord*, as displayed by his faithful ministers, have subdued their *thousands*, and the riches of his grace their *ten thousands*, when illustrated by those who have not only heard, but have themselves tasted of their sweetness. *The preaching of the cross* may indeed *to them that perish* be *foolishness;* but blessed be his name who died upon it, there is still a happy remnant, to whom it appears to be *the power of God, and the wisdom of God.* 1 Cor. i. 18, 24.

Evangelical subjects, when opened with perspicuity, and enforced with vigor and tenderness, by those that have experienced the transforming energy of them on their own hearts, and desire above all things, to be *wise to win* the *souls* of others, (Prov. xi. 30,) are generally the occasion of producing the most immediate and the most important change; as I doubt not, but many now present have seen and felt. And the observation of every year of life convinces me more and more that they who desire to be signally instrumental in this good work—this work of all others the most benevolent and important—must, in the account of a vain world, *become fools, that they may be wise.* 1 Cor. iii. 18. How contemptuously soever it may be fashionable to treat such preaching, we must make these subjects familiar to our hearers, and must treat them with all plainness of speech, and all seriousness of address, or we shall generally *labor in vain, and spend our strength for nought.* Isa. xlix. 4.

Would to God, that the teachers of our Israel may consider the importance of it, and grow wise by such experiments as these! that they may act the part of prudent physicians, who prescribe the medicines they find in fact most useful, and not those concerning which the finest speculations may be framed. Till then, whatever their learning, politeness, and parade may be, it cannot be expected that our health should be generally recovered; but we are like to continue, what we have long been, a vicious people, amidst the finest encomiums of virtue, that are anywhere to be found: nor will there be much room to wonder, if some of its most eloquent advocates should appear, even in their own practice, insensible of those charms which they so gracefully recommend to others, and sink in their character below those heathen moralists, whom they may choose to imitate, rather than Christ and his apostles. Nevertheless, I am persuaded, that if God intend mercy for us as a people, he will support among us a succession of those who shall dispense his truths in such a manner, as he has generally chosen to honor with success. But though the greater part of sincere converts are won by these, I am to add,

2. That remarkable providences, whether merciful or afflictive, are occasions which God takes to work upon the hearts of many others.

When ordinary means have long been attended in vain, God perhaps interposes, by other more peculiar and signal methods, to *pluck* the trifling and lethargic sinner *as a firebrand out of the burning.* Amos iv. 11.

Sometimes remarkable mercies and deliverances accomplish the work. An appearance of God in their favor, when they are conscious to themselves that they are the unworthiest of all his creatures, shall shame and melt them, and powerfully prevail on their minds to *turn unto the*

Lord, who *daily loads them with his benefits;* (Ps. lxviii. 19;) and thus seems, in more senses than one, to send from heaven to save them, and to *draw them out of many waters*, in which they had otherwise been lost. Ps. xviii. 16.

But we more frequently see, that afflictions are the means of performing this happy work. By a gracious severity God is pleased to lay hold on many, and to give them reason to bless the hand, which, though by a rough motion, delivers them from the flames that were kindling around them, and shows the Lord to be *merciful to them.* Gen. xix. 16. Like Jonah in the ship, they are awakened by *a storm to call upon their God:* (John i. 6:) like Manasseh, they are *taken among the thorns, and laid in fetters*, that they may be brought *to know the Lord:* (2 Chron. xxxiii. 11, 13:) like the jailer, they are shaken with *an earthquake*, and *trembling and astonished* they *fall down*, and inquire *what they shall do to be saved.* Acts xvi. 26–30. The terrifying fear of the approach of death, or the distressing weight of some calamity, which threatens every moment to swallow them up in destruction, rouses their consciences to an attention to those divine truths which they had long forgotten, and opens those records of guilt which they had studiously sealed up.

And there seems to be no affliction by which God more frequently works upon men than by sickness. When he weakens their capacity for the business of life, and spoils their relish for its enjoyments; when he confines them to their chambers, or even to their beds, and *makes their chain straight* and *heavy;* (Lam. iii. 7;) when he threatens *to take them away in the midst of their days,* (Psal. xii. 24,) *to deprive them of the residue of their years,* (Isa. xxiii. 10,) and immediately to bring them before that awful tribunal, for which they know, in their own consciences, they are so ill prepared: then do we often see the accomplishment of that observation which Elihu made so many ages ago; *He chasteneth a man with pain upon his bed, and the multitude of his bones with strong pain, so that his life abhorreth bread, and his soul dainty meat: his flesh is consumed away that it cannot be seen: and his bones, that were not seen, stick out; yea, his soul draweth near to the grave, and his life to the destroyers:* but sending him *an interpreter, one among a thousand, to show unto man his uprightness, then he is gracious to him, and saith,* in a spiritual as well as literal sense, *Deliver him from going down to the pit, I have found a ransom.* Job xxxiii. 19–24. Blessed be God, instances of this kind have been known among us, in which the sickness of the body has wrought the cure of the soul, under the conduct of the great Physician of both; and so has proved eminently to the glory of God, and the good of those who, *for a while, have been in heaviness.* 1 Pet. i. 6.

Yet it must be acknowledged, that, in other instances, the remorse which a man expresses upon a sick bed, and in the near views of eternity, proves but like that of some condemned malefactor, who, when he has obtained a pardon, throws off all those appearances of repentance with which he had once deceived himself, and perhaps deceived others too, and plunges himself anew into capital crime; it may be, into crimes for which he afterwards suffers death, without those compunctions of conscience which he before felt, being hardened by a return into sin, attended with such dreadful aggravations. This has been the case of many; and I pray God it may not be thus with any of you.

But if there be any among you that were once under powerful awakenings; and that have cried out of *terrors on every side;* (Job xviii. 11;) that have confessed your sins, it may be, with greater freedom, and a more particular detail of circumstances, than the minister who attended you could have desired, and have resolved against them with all the appearances of the most determined purpose; and yet, after all, have *returned with the sow that was washed, to her wallowing in the mire:* (2 Pet. ii. 22:) such have peculiar reason to be alarmed and terrified. Every day of Divine patience toward such is astonishing. And if to all this have been added the returns of danger, and signal interposition of Providence for your deliverance, and yet there be no kindly impressions of penitence and gratitude on your hearts, they who know the particulars of the case, must surely look upon you with horror as well as with wonder: for what can one imagine of such, but that they are given over by God to a darkness, which nothing but the flames of hell can enlighten, and a hardness, which nothing can penetrate but the sharpness of unquenchable fire, and the gnawings of the never-dying worm?

But to return from a digression, into which compassion towards such a deplorable case has insensibly led me, I would farther observe, that as these various interpositions of a remarkable Providence are often the means of working saving impressions on men's minds, so,

3. God is sometimes pleased to overrule little and inconsiderable incidents in life, as the occasion of accomplishing this happy change.

As the treasure of the Gospel was at first put *into earthen vessels, that the excellency of the power might* appear to *be of God, and not of man;* (2 Cor. iv. 6;) so God to *make his* own *praise glorious,* (Psal. lxvi. 2,) is sometimes pleased to produce the most important effects, by causes which seem in themselves least considerable. And it is astonishing to see from how small and seemingly unpromising a seed this plant of paradise springs up, and with how little cultivation too in some instances, after *Paul* had long attempted in vain to *plant,* and *Apollos* to *water.* 1 Cor. iii. 6, 7. A few lines in the Bible, or any other good book, perhaps taken up by chance, shall be the instrument; and a passage, on which the eye glances without expectation or design, shall strike to the heart, like an arrow from the bow of God himself—after quivers of the most pointed and polished shafts have been exhausted in vain, though such shafts were most skillfully aimed, and most vigorously discharged. In other instances, a word dropped in conversation, and that perhaps no way remarkable either for its spirit or propriety, shall do that which the most solemn ordinances have not been capable of doing: an important encouragement, by the way, to abound in religious discourse, which God has sometimes been pleased to honor as the happy *means of saving a soul from death,* and laying a foundation for the delights of an everlasting friendship with those who have been so recovered.

4. Sometimes this great work is accomplished by secret and immediate impressions from God upon the mind, without any visible means, instruments, or occasions at all.

These things do not frequently happen; nor does it seem fit they should, lest any should be encouraged to expect them in the neglect of the appointed means. Nevertheless, it is plain, in fact, that God is sometimes pleased to go out of the common way; and his mighty hand is to be acknowledged in it. The reasons are known to himself; and the praise is humbly to be ascribed to him *who giveth not an account of any of his matters.* Job. xxxiii. 13.

It is not, to be sure, so common now as it was in the days of Elihu, that God should *speak to men in a dream,* or *seal instruction* to them *in slumberings on their bed;* (Job xxxiii. 15, 16 ;) yet I have myself known several who have ascribed their first religious awakenings to some awful dream, in which the solemnity of the judgment day, or a view of the invisible world, has been represented to them with unspeakable terror; and others, to whom, when they have waked in the night, some words of scripture have occurred with such power, that they have not been able to divert their thoughts to anything else; and that when they themselves have not certainly known whether they were in the Bible or not.

I have known those that, in the circle of their vain companions, and in the midst of their sensual delights, have been struck to the very heart with some such scripture as this: *to be carnally minded is death:* (Rom. viii. 6:) or such a text as this has, on a sudden, darted into their minds; *The wrath of God is revealed from heaven against all ungodliness and unrighteousness of men.* Rom. i. 18. Such passages have seemed to ring and thunder in their ears, till the sound of their music, and the noise of their mirth have been quite overpowered, so that they have been driven from their revels to their knees, and have returned no more into *the paths of the destroyer.*

Yea, to add no more instances of this kind, I have known those of distinguished genius, polite manners, and great experience in human affairs, who, after having outgrown all the impressions of a religious education; after having been hardened, rather than subdued, by the most singular mercies, even various, repeated, and astonishing deliverances, which have appeared to themselves no less than miraculous; after having lived for years *without God in the world,* notoriously corrupt themselves, and laboring to the utmost to corrupt others; have been stopped on a sudden in the full career of their sin, and have felt such rays of the Divine presence, and of redeeming love, darting in upon their minds, almost *like lightning from heaven*, as have at once roused, overpowered, and transformed them; so that they have come out of their chambers with an irreconcilable enmity to those vices, to which, when they entered them, they were the tamest and most abandoned slaves; and have appeared, from that very hour, the votaries, the patrons, the champions of religion; and after a course of the most resolute attachment to it, in spite of all the reasonings, or the railleries, the importunities, or the reproaches of its enemies, they have continued to this day some of its brightest ornaments: a change which I behold with equal wonder and delight, and which, if a nation should join in deriding it, I would adore as *the finger of God.**

In mentioning these things thus publicly, I do indeed take an uncommon freedom, which some may perhaps censure; but so far as human testimony can give an assurance of truth, I may justly say, that *I speak what I know, and testify what*, in its genuine and powerful effects, *I have* myself *seen.* John iii. 11. And since the possi-

* The conversion of Col. Gardiner is evidently alluded to here, in which Dr. Doddridge was deeply interested.—J. N. B.

bility of abusing such condescensions of Divine mercy did not prevent their being granted, I can not think it ought to engage me to be silent, when so natural an opportunity offered of declaring them, *to the glory of him who worketh all things according to the counsel of his own will.* Ephes. i. 11. Yet I must repeat the caution which I before suggested, that it would be madness for any to neglect God's appointed means of operation, on presumption that they shall be added to the small list of those who have been such uncommon and astonishing trophies of the efficacy and sovereignty of Divine grace.

These remarks must for the present suffice, with regard to the various occasions by which God works upon men's minds.* And I hope you will excuse me, if in illustrating some of them, I have a little anticipated some things which might have been mentioned under the third head, in which I proposed,

III. To consider some varieties observable in the manner in which Divine grace operates on the mind.

And this variety, by the way, will be observ-

* It is well to notice that the revealed word of God is in all these different modes of application the powerful instrument. This is the only safeguard against delusions of all kinds.—J. N. B.

able in many instances where the occasions are in general the same. Thus among those that are awakened by the word of God, or by his providence, some are shaken by *strong terrors*, some are melted into *deep sorrows;* others are astonished, as it were, and captivated at once, by the discovery of *the love of God in Christ*, and others are led on by such *gentle and gradual impressions*, that they can hardly recollect any remarkable circumstance at all relating to the manner in which this blessed work was begun, or conducted in their souls.

1. Some converts are awakened by strong terrors.

It is obvious, that conviction of sin, in some degree or other, is absolutely necessary to make way for the entrance of the gospel into the soul. But the degrees are various in different persons; and as for those of whom we now speak, God *reproves them* aloud *and sets their sins in order before them*, (Psal. l. 21,) marshals them in dreadful array, as the expression imports; so that they seem like defenceless criminals surrounded by a host of enemies, whose weapons are raised for their destruction. Yea, God himself, the great, the terrible, the eternal, and omnipotent God, seems to *set them up as a mark for those arrows*, (Lam. iii. 12,) *the poison of which drinketh up their spirits:* (Job. vi. 4:) and, as he himself expresses it, *He is unto them as a bear* or *a lion,* ready to tear and *rend the* very *caul of their heart.* Hos. xiii. 8.

They *come,* as it were, to the trembling and terrifying *Mount Sinai,* to *blackness, and darkness, and tempest.* Heb. xii. 18. The conviction of guilt is attended with such a sense of the demerit of sin, as fills them with horror and astonishment, and engages them to wish *in the bitterness of their souls,* that they had *never been born.* They are left for a time, and that perhaps for weeks and months, to be, as it were, deafened with the loud thunders of the law; *a dreadful sound,* as Eliphaz expresses it, *is in their ears,* (Job. xv. 21,) even the sentence of their own damnation; and the awful curse of an almighty, sin-avenging God *comes into their bowels like water, and like oil into their bones.* Psal. cix. 18.

They are filled with such deep remorse for their past sins, that they verily think no iniquity was ever like theirs, and that no punishment will be like theirs. They hardly see a glimmering of hope that they shall obtain deliverance, but expect, in a very little while, to be sealed up under wrath, if they are not already so. When they hear the offers and the promises of the Gospel, they can apply none of them to themselves, and find comfort in none: but every threatening and every curse of the book of God seems to have been written as their intended portion. And thus, perhaps, they continue for weeks or for months together, expecting every day and every night that *destruction from God,* which is now a *terror to them.* (Job xxxi. 23,) should utterly *swallow them up*, and *leave them neither root nor branch,* neither comfort nor hope. Mal. iv. 1. *The law is a schoolmaster to bring them to Christ,* (Gal. iii. 24,) and it scourges them with the most rigorous discipline; yea, the infernal lion roars over them, though he is not permitted to devour them: he particularly terrifies them when they think of approaching God, as if they were to meet with some peculiar danger there, where alone they can find their relief: or, if they do in broken accents utter their prayer before God, it seems to be *shut out,* (Lam. iii. 8,) and they are apprehensive that it is *turned into sin.* Psal. cix. 7. Yet there is one thing to be observed in the midst of this scene of horror, and it is a circumstance of great importance, that they justify God when he seems most inexorable, and subscribe to that sentence as righteous which dooms them to eternal ruin.

2. Others are melted into deep sorrows.

Their *eyes run down with tears;* and they are ready to wish that their *head were waters, and* their *eyes fountains, that they might* continue to *weep day and night.* Jer. ix. 1, 18. They see the evil of sin, and the misery to which it has reduced them, in a most deplorable view; and it may be, while those described under the former head are ready to tremble because they can not weep ; these are ready to weep because they cannot tremble. They lament, among other things, the want of those strong horrors which some have felt : they cry out, "*Woe is me! for I am undone ;* (Isa. vi. 5 ;) I have *destroyed myself,* and in myself my *help* is not found." Hos. xiii. 9.

It may be, indeed, a considerable time before they can persuade themselves there is any help for them even in God. They know there is help in him through Christ for penitent and believing sinners : but they cannot easily be convinced that they believe, because they do not feel that confident trust which some others have much sooner been brought to ; and they are afraid, lest whatever they experience, which looks like repentance, should be only the false appearance of it, proceeding from mere self-love and a natural dread of future misery. They dwell perpetually on the dark side of things : they read over the catalogue of their iniquities again and again, and attend to those passages in which *the wrath of God is revealed from heaven against* every kind and degree of *sin;* (Rom. i. 18;) while they are slow of heart to admit those reviving consolations which the various rich and precious promises of the Gospel are so admirably well calculated to administer.

The state of such souls, when they are first savingly enlightened, is like that of the earth, when fogs and mists have vailed the face of the sun after it is risen. But it very often happens, with respect to such souls, that when these mists are at length dispersed, a very bright and cheerful day opens: they are comforted by the warmer beams of the *Sun of Righteousness*, according to the hours in which they have been beclouded, and are *made glad according to the days in which* they were *afflicted:* (Psal. xc. 15:) and going on *to fear the Lord*, and to *obey the voice of his servant*, though they have long *walked in darkness, and seen no light*, they are at length encouraged by his Spirit enforcing the exhortations of his word, to *trust in the name of the Lord, and stay themselves upon their God.* Isa. l. 10.

3. Some are captivated with astonishing and delightful views of the love of God in Christ.

There is always, as we observed before, in the awakened soul, some conviction of sin and apprehension of danger; nevertheless, there are instances in which God heals almost as soon as he wounds, and speaks peace almost as soon as he speaks trouble. He graciously shortens, to some souls, the pangs of the new birth, and *gives them beauty for ashes, the oil of joy for mourning, and the garment of praise for the spirit of heaviness.* Isa. lxi. 3. The news of salvation by the blood, and righteousness, and grace of Christ, is received with so thankful a sense, with so joyful a compliance, that the soul, feeling beyond all doubt the cordial sincerity with which it embraces the offer, is filled with *joy unspeakable, and full of glory:* (1 Pet. i. 8:) the heart *does magnify the Lord, and the spirit rejoices in God the Saviour.* Luke i. 46, 47.

This was remarkably the case of the jailer, who in the very night in which he was converted, that same night in which the foundation of his house had been shaken, and his own soul too shaken, by an earthquake, so that he had endeavored to lay violent hands on himself: yet, I say, that very night, before the day appeared, having been directed to *believe on the Lord Jesus Christ,* that he might *be saved,* and been enabled, by Divine grace to comply with the exhortation, it is added concerning him, that *he rejoiced, believing in God with all his house.* Acts xvi. 34. Thus too the Thessalonians, though they *received the word in much affliction,* and ran the risk of losing their possessions and their lives in adhering to it, yet received it *with joy of the Holy Ghost.* 1 Thes. i. 6. And though I cannot say this is God's most ordinary way of dealing, and though I fear the counterfeit appearance of such a work as this often leaves men in the number of those whom our Lord represents by *stony ground hearers;* (Matt. xiii. 20, 21;) yet it is certain, some instances of this kind are still to be found. But then I must observe, this is a joy attended with the deepest humility, and animates the soul to the most ardent and affectionate resolution of *walking worthy of the Lord unto all pleasing, being strengthened with all might, according to his glorious power, unto all patience and long-suffering with joyfulness.* Col. i. 10, 11.

4. Others—and these perhaps the greatest part of such as are religiously educated—are led on by such gentle and insensible degrees, that they can hardly recollect any remarkable circumstances that have attended their conversion, nor can certainly fix on the particular time of it.

God is sometimes, in the preceding instances, *in the whirlwind, the earthquake, and the fire;* but he is also frequently *in the still small voice.* 1 Kings xix. 11, 12. The operations of the Holy Spirit on the soul are often, and perhaps generally, of such a nature, that it is difficult exactly to distinguish them from the rational exercise of our own thoughts, because the Spirit operates by suggesting rational views of things, and awakening rational affections. For whatever some have vainly and dangerously insinuated, nothing is so rational as the sentiments and temper which prevail in renewed souls, and to which it is the work of God's regenerating Spirit to bring them.

These operations, where there is a religious education, often begin very early: but then, in some degree, the impressions wear off from the weak and flexible mind; and perhaps there are various instances in which they alternately revive and decay again. And this vicissitude of affectionate applications to religion under moving ordinances, afflictions, or deliverances, and of backslidings and remissness in it, with respect to many, may be permitted to continue for a long time. At length, under the various methods of Providence and Grace, the soul attains to greater steadiness, and a more habitual victory over the remains of indwelling sin: but it may be exceeding hard, and perhaps absolutely impossible, to determine concerning some remarkable scenes through which it has passed, whether such a one in particular, perhaps the last which strikes the memory, were the season of its new birth; or whether it were merely a recovery from such a degree of negligence and remissness, as may possibly be consistent with real religion, and be found in a regenerate soul.

These balancings of backsliding and recovery often occasion very great perplexity; and such sort of converts are frequently much discouraged, because they cannot give the history of their religious experiences in so elear and distinct a manner as others: and particularly, because they have not passed through such violent terrors and agitations of mind as many, who were perhaps once sunk into much deeper degeneracy have done. Nevertheless, where there is a consciousness of an undissembled love to God, an unreserved devotedness to his service, a cordial trust in the Lord Jesus Christ, and a sincere affection to mankind in general, and especially to *those of the household of faith*, a man ought not to perplex himself on this account. For as every man knows he was born into the world, by a consciousness that he now lives and acts here, though it is impossible he should remember anything of the time or circumstances in which he was first introduced into it; so may a Christian be assured, that some way or another he was *born of the Spirit*, if he can trace its genuine fruits and efficacious influences in a renewed heart and life.

I have thus laid down several particulars. which

appeared to me important, in order to illustrate that diversity which is observable in the methods of the Divine operations on the heart; and they will naturally lead us to these three reflections, with which I shall conclude my present Discourse. Let us not make *our own experiences* a standard for *others*;—nor the *experiences of others* a standard for *ourselves*;—nor let us be unwilling, in a prudent manner, to *communicate* our spiritual experiences to each other.

1. Let us not make our own experiences a standard for others.

Let us remember that there is, as we have heard, *a diversity of operations;* and that many a person may be a dear child of God, who was not born just with those circumstances which attended our own regeneration. Others may not so particularly have discerned the time, the occasion, the progress of the change; they may not have felt all that we have felt, either in the way of extraordinary terror or extraordinary comfort; and yet, perhaps, may equal, or even exceed us in that holy temper, to which it was the great intention of our Heavenly Father, by one method or another, to bring all his children. Nay, I will add, that Christians of a very amiable and honorable character may express themselves but in a dark, and something of an improper manner, concerning the doctrine of regeneration, and may, in conscience, scruple the use of some phrases relating to it, which we judge to be exceeding suitable; and yet, that very scruple which displeases us may proceed from a reverence for God and truth, and from such a tenderness of heart as is the effect of his renewing grace. We should therefore be very cautious how we judge each other, and take upon us to reject those whom perhaps God has received.

I remember good Dr. Owen, whose candor was, in many respects, very remarkable, carries this so far, as somewhere to say, "that some may, perhaps, have experienced the saving influences of the Holy Spirit on their hearts, who do not in words acknowledge the necessity, or even the reality of those influences." Judging men's hearts, and judging their states, is a work for which we are so ill qualified, that we have reason to be exceeding thankful it is not assigned to us. And when we are entering into such an examination of their character, as our duty may in some particular circumstances seem to require, we should be very solicitous that we do not lay down arbitrary and precarious rules. It seems, indeed, that so far as we can learn it, we may more safely judge by their present temper and conduct, than by the history of anything which has formerly passed in their minds.

And let me add it as a necessary caution here, that they who never felt any of the extraordinary emotions of mind, which have been described under some former heads, but have been brought to religion by less observable methods, perhaps by calm, rational views of it—of whom I believe there are great numbers—should be very cautious that they do not rashly censure such things as I have now been representing, as if they were mere enthusiasm. I can not but think this a criminal *limiting the Holy One of Israel,* (Psal. lxxviii. 41,) and fear it will be found a boldness highly displeasing to him, and very injurious to the souls of those who allow themselves in it, and of others too, if they be such as are employed in the ministerial work: not now to insist on what, in comparison of this, is but a small matter, the apparent rudeness and petulance of contradicting facts so well attested as many of this kind have been, and running counter to the solid effects which such impressions have produced. The rashness which prevails under different forms among men of the most opposite sentiments, is too obvious; but if we would give ourselves leave calmly to weigh and consider matters, our spirits would be rendered on all sides more moderate, and many harsh and hasty censures would be suspended, which at present prove very little more than the ignorance, pride, and folly of those that pass them.

2. Let us not make the experiences of others a standard for ourselves.

This is frequently the case, and especially with those who are naturally of an humble and tender temper; for whose peace and comfort therefore one can not but be peculiarly solicitous. Having heard of some extraordinary experiences of others, they are ready to imagine, because they can trace nothing correspondent to these in their own minds, that they are utter strangers to real regeneration, and have nothing more than such religious notions and forms, as natural men may easily learn of each other.

But what I have now been saying of the variety of the Divine operations on the heart, affords a solid answer to such scruples, when they arise in a pious mind. Reflect, on this occasion, how it is in the works of nature: there we know that God works in all, so that he is the life and existence of the whole creation; and yet, as an excellent writer expresses it, "He alone seems not to work." His agency is so invisible and secret, that did not reason and scripture join to teach it, one might live a great many years in the world without knowing anything more, than that such and such effects are produced by correspondent second causes: though in strict propriety of speech they are no causes at all, but owe all their efficacy to the Divine presence and operation. Sense tells us that the sun enlightens the earth, and warms it; that the rain waters it, the seeds produce vegetables, and the animals continue their proper race; but that God is *the Father of lights*, (Jam. i. 17,) that he *has prepared the light and the sun:* (Psal. lxxiv. 16;) that he *visits the earth, and causes rain to descend into the furrows thereof*, (Ps. lxv. 9, 10,) so as to *make the grass to grow for cattle*, and corn *and herb for the service of man;* (Psal. civ. 14;) that he *sends forth his Spirit*, and the animal race is *created*, and *the face of the earth renewed;* (Psal. civ. 30;) this, I say, is what multitudes of the human race are not aware of; because in all these things he acts in a gentle, stated, and regular manner, and employs inferior agents as the instruments of his providence. And just thus gentle, silent, and regular are the influences of his Spirit upon men's souls; and it is often impossible exactly to distinguish them from the teachings of parents and ministers, and from those reflections which seem to spring from our own minds, though it is *he that gives us counsel*, while *our reins instruct us* in our secret musings, (Psal. xvi. 7,) and that teaches us to profit by the lessons which others give us.

Be not therefore surprised, and be not dejected, though you cannot assign the place, the time, the manner, in which your conversion began; and though you are strangers to the terrors, the sorrows, or the transports of joy, which you have heard one and another express. *The wind bloweth where it listeth,* and the Spirit dispenses his influences where and when, and in what measure and degree he pleases; but while the way and manner of his operation may be secret and unknown, the effects of it are sensible and evident; and as with regard to the *wind, thou hearest the sound thereof, but canst not tell whence it cometh, and whither it goeth; so is every one that is born of the Spirit.* John iii. 8. You may not certainly know when to fix the precise time of your conversion, or how to trace the particular steps by which it has been brought to pass; for *as thou knowest not what is the way of the Spirit, nor how the bones do grow in the womb of her that is with child; even so thou knowest not the works of God who maketh all.* Eccl. xi. 5. But though you cannot trace the process of the operation, the effects of it are such as you may feel within you, and *by its fruits* it will be *known.* Matt. vii. 20.

It is indeed desirable to be able to give an account of the beginning and the progress of the work of God upon your souls, as some that are regenerate can do; but this is not necessary to evidence the truth of grace. Happy is he who in this case can say as the blind man in the gospel, *One thing I know, that whereas I was blind, now I see.* John ix. 25. For as you know that there is fire when you see the flame, though you know not how or when it began; so also it may be discerned, that you have really undergone a saving change, though you know not how or when it was wrought in your hearts. If you answer the characters I laid down in the preceding discourses, as essential to the truly regenerate, which are all comprehended in repentance and faith, producing an unfeigned love and uniform obedience, you may trace the cause from the effect, with far greater certainty than you could have traced such an effect, as what would infallibly follow from any cause which you could have perceived in your minds previous to it. There may be great awakenings, violent terrors, and ecstatic joys, where there is no saving work of God on the soul; but where the Divine image is produced, and the soul is actually renewed, we are sure, as was before observed, that grace has been working, though we know not when, or where, or how.

And therefore, on the whole, guarding against both these extremes, and to cure them both,

3. Let Christians, in a prudent and humble manner, be ready to communicate their religious experiences to each other.

God undoubtedly intended that the variety of his operations should be observed and owned in the world of grace, as well as in that of nature; and as these things pass in the secret recesses of men's hearts, how should they be known, unless they will themselves communicate and declare them? And let me caution you against that strange averseness to all freedoms of this kind, which, especially in persons of a reserved temper, is so ready to prevail.

Let not any think it beneath them to do it. You well know that David, who was not only a a man of an admirable genius, but a mighty prince, too, was far from thinking it so; on the contrary, deeply impressed with the Divine condescension in all the gracious visits he had received from him, he calls, as it were, the whole pious world around him, that they might be edified and comforted by the relation: *Come*, says he, *and hear, all ye that fear God, and I will declare what he has done for my soul.* Psal. lxvi. 16. He proclaimed it, not with his voice and harp alone, but with his immortal pen; and many other noble and excellent persons concurred with him; and the invaluable treasure of their experiences, in as great a variety of circumstances as we can well imagine, is transmitted to us in the book of Psalms. Can any just reason then be assigned, why they, who live under a nobler dispensation, and a more abundant communication of the Spirit, should be entirely silent on this subject?

There may indeed be an over-forwardness, which is the apparent effect of pride and self-conceit, and which, with thinking people, may bring even the sincerity of the speaker into question, or put his indiscretion beyond all possibility of being questioned. But it would be very unreasonable to argue, that because a thing may be done ill, it cannot possibly be done well.

Why may not intimate friends open their hearts to each other on such delightful topics? Why may not they, who have met with anything peculiar of this kind, communicate it to their minister? And though I must in conscience declare against making it absolutely and universally a term of communion, yet I am well assured that in some instances a prudent and serious communication of these things to a Christian society, when a person is to be admitted into fellowship with it, has often answered very valuable ends.

By this means God has the honor of his own work: and others have the pleasure of sympathizing with the relator, both in his sorrows and his joys: they derive from hence some additional satisfaction as to his fitness for an approach to the Lord's table; they learn with pleasure the Divine blessing which attends the administration of ordinances among them: and make observations and remarks which may assist them in offering their addresses to God, and in giving proper advices to others who are in circumstances like those related. To all which we may add, that the ministers of Christ do, in particular, learn what may be a means of forming them to a more experimental manner of preaching, as well as in many instances discover those, before unknown, tokens of success which may strengthen their hands in the work of their great Master.

It is by frequent conversations of this kind, I have learned many of the particulars on which I have grounded the preceding discourse. I hope therefore you will excuse me, if, on so natural an occasion, I have borne my public testimony to what has been so edifying to me, both as a minister and a Christian. And the tender regard which I have for young persons training up for the work of the ministry, and my ardent desire that they may learn the language of Zion, and have those peculiar advantages which nothing but an acquaintance with causes, and an observation on facts can give, has been a further inducement to me to add this reflection, with which I conclude my discourse; humbly hoping that what you have heard upon this occasion will, by the Divine blessing, furnish out agreeable matter for such conversation as I have now recommended, to the glory of God, and to the advancement of religion among you. *Amen.*

DISCOURSE IX.

DIRECTIONS TO AWAKENED SINNERS.

ACTS IX. 6.

And he, trembling and astonished, said, Lord, what wilt thou have me to do?

THESE are the words of Saul, *who also is called Paul,* (Acts xiii. 9,) when he was stricken to the ground as he was going to Damascus; and any one who had looked upon him in his present circumstances and knew nothing more of him than that view, in comparison with his past life, could have given, would have imagined him one of the most miserable creatures that ever lived upon earth, and would have expected that he should very soon have been numbered among the most miserable of those in hell.

He was engaged in a course of such savage cruelty as can upon no principle of common morality be vindicated, even though the Christians had been as much mistaken, as he rashly and foolishly concluded they were. After having *dragged many of them into prison*, and *given his voice against* some *that were put to death*, he *persecuted* others *into strange cities;* and had now *obtained a commission from the Sanhedrim at Jerusalem* to carry this holy, or rather this impious war into *Damascus*, (Acts xxvi. 10–12,) and to bring all the disciples of the blessed Jesus bound from thence to Jerusalem: (Acts ix. 2:) probably that they might there be animadverted upon with greater severity than could safely have been attempted by the Jews in so distant a city, under a foreign governor.

But behold, *as he was in the way*, Jesus interposes, clothed with a lustre exceeding that of the *sun at noon.* Acts xxvi. 13. He strikes him down from the beast on which he rode, and lays him prostrate on the ground, calling to him with a voice far more dreadful than that of thunder, *Saul, Saul, why persecutest thou me?* Acts ix. 4.

Any one would have imagined, from the circumstances in which he now beheld Saul, that Divine vengeance had already begun to seize him, and that full execution would quickly have been done. But *God's ways are not as our ways, nor are his thoughts as our thoughts.* Isa. lv. 8. Christ laid him almost as low as hell, that he might raise him as high as the third heaven; of which he afterwards gave him a view in vision, to anticipate his reception into it. 2 Cor. xii. 2. This day of his terror and astonishment was, in a nobler sense than any other, the day of his birth; for he is brought to bow himself at the foot of an injured Saviour, to offer him, as it were, a blank upon which to write his own terms of peace; and as soon as he heard that this glorious person was *Jesus, whom*, in his members, *he* had so long *persecuted*, he makes his submission in these lively, comprehensive words, *Lord, what wilt thou have me to do?* This was not a time for a long speech; but he that discerns all the secret recesses of the spirit, knew these few words were full of a most important meaning, and expressed not only a grief of heart for all that he had before been doing against Christ and his kingdom, but the sincerest resolution for the future to employ himself in his service, waiting only the intimations of his wise and gracious will, as to the most proper and acceptable manner of beginning the attempt.

There is, methinks, a poignant kind of eloquence in this short expression, far beyond what any paraphrase upon it can give: and our compassionate Lord accepted this surrender. All his former rebellions were no more remembered against him; and before he rose from the ground, to which he fell on so terrible an occasion, Christ gave him an intimation, not only that his forfeited life should be spared, so that he should get safe into the city to which he was bound, but that he should there be instructed in the service which Jesus, whom he had persecuted, would now condescend to receive at his hands.

I represent the case thus largely, because I hope it is a case, which, in some measure, suits the experience of some that hear me this evening. Paul tells us, it was *for this reason*, among others, that he himself *obtained mercy*, though he was *the chief of sinners, that in him, as the chief, Jesus Christ might show forth all long-suffering, for a pattern to them who should afterwards believe.* 1 Tim. i. 15, 16.

Is there then, in this assembly, any awakened and convinced sinner; any one that, apprized of his folly, and sensible of his misery, is desirous to fall at the foot of Christ, and say with Saul, *Lord, what wilt thou have me to do? That which I see not, teach thou me; and wherein I have done iniquity, I will do so no more!* Job xxxiv. 32. Such would I now especially address; and while I put the question, Is there any such among us? I would fain persuade myself, there are several. For I humbly hope, that all the labors that have been bestowed in the preceding discourses are not in vain, nor all the prayers that have been offered for their success in vain; prayers which,

I doubt not, have been carried by many of you into your families and your closets, as well as jointly presented to God in this public assembly. Trusting, therefore, that it is thus with some, and praying that it may be a more frequent case, I proceed,

Sixthly, to give some directions to such as are awakened by Divine grace to a sense of their misery in an unregenerate state, and are brought to desire recovery from it.

To such I propose to give directions: and to what purpose would it be to undertake to offer them to any others? Who would pretend to teach those who are unconcerned about their salvation, what methods they are to take in order to their becoming truly regenerate? This, methinks, would be like giving directions how those might learn to write who do not desire it, and will not take a pen into their hands. All I could say to such, while they continue in this character, would vanish into empty air. It would not, probably, be so much as observed and remembered.

I speak therefore to awakened souls, and it is pleasant to address such on this head. Ananias undoubtedly undertook his message to Saul with cheerfulness, to tell him what Christ would have him to do: and I would with pleasure and cheerfulness engage in the like work; humbly hoping, that some will hear with observation and attention—will hear for themselves and so *hear for their good.* Job v. 27. And to this purpose let me advise you—to attend to the impressions that have been made upon you with great seriousness—to break off everything that is contrary to them—to seek for further knowledge in religious matters—to pour out your souls before God in earnest prayer—to communicate the state of your case to some experienced Christian—to acquaint yourselves with such as are much in your own circumstances—to fly immediately to Christ, as ready to receive all that come to him—to dedicate yourselves to him, and to his service, in the most solemn manner—to arm yourselves to encounter the greatest difficulties in your Christian course—and finally, to take every step in this attempt with a deep sense of your own weakness, and an humble dependence upon Divine grace to be communicated to you as the matter requires. These are the several directions I would offer to you: and may they be impressed in such a manner on your souls, that none of you may *lose the things* that have been *wrought:* (2 John ver. 8:) but by the effectual *working* of the *mighty power of God,* (Eph. i. 19,) such as he graciously has been pleased to *bring to the birth,* may be *brought forth*, (Isa. lxvi. 9,) and such as are awakened may be savingly renewed!

1. I would advise you to *attend* to the impressions made upon you with great seriousness.

They may perhaps take you a little off the world and its concernments; and some will blame you for suffering such an interruption: but regard not that censure. The time will come, if you pursue these things aright, when renewed diligence, prudence, and the Divine blessing, will amply make amends for any present hindrance which these impressions may occasion. And if it should be otherwise, *is there not a cause?* If a man seized with a threatening distemper should choose, for a little while, to lay aside his usual business, that he might attend to the care of his health, before the symptoms grew incurable would any body blame him for this? On the contrary, would it not be looked upon as acting a very wise, prudent, and necessary part? Much more may be said here. *It is not a light thing for you, because it is your life.* Deut. xxxii. 47. And if *the life is more than meat, and the body than raiment*, (Matt. vi. 25,) then surely the soul is more to be regarded than either. And therefore what you do in your worldly affairs, do moderately, and do not grudge that retirement which is so necessary in such a tender circumstance as this.

I may apply to you, on this occasion, those words of Solomon: *Through desire a man having separated himself, seeketh and intermeddleth with all wisdom.* Prov. xviii. 1. If you desire to attain Divine wisdom, you must separate yourself from all other things to pursue it. And it is the more necessary to attend to this now, because the Tempter may probably contrive to lay some more than ordinary avocation in your way, at a time when the interest of his kingdom requires you should be diverted from prosecuting those views which are presenting themselves to you, and by which you may so probably be rescued out of his hands, and put forever out of his power.

2. Let me advise you to break off everything which is contrary to such impressions as these.

Sin will immediately appear to have been your disease and your ruin: and therefore, if ever you hope for recovery, you must resolutely break with that; not merely with this or that particular evil, but with every sin; and that not only for a little while, but entirely and forever. A mortal, irreconcilable war must be declared against it. Every fleshly lust must be denied, every immoral practice, for which your heart may at any time smite you, must be reformed; and if ever you expect to reap mercy and life, you must, as the prophet expresses it, *break up your fallow ground*, (Hos. x. 12,) and *not sow among thorns*. Jer. iv. 3. For *righteousness has no fellowship with unrighteousness, and light no communion with darkness.* 2 Cor. vi. 14. And you may be assured, that as all sin grieves the Spirit of God, and strengthens the heavy fetters which lie upon the soul; so those sins which are committed after these awakenings and convictions, have a peculiar guilt attending them, and do greater *despite to the Spirit of grace*, (Heb. x. 29,) in proportion to the degree in which his motions on the soul have been vigorous and warm.

3. Seek further *knowledge*, especially from the word and ordinances of God.

The influences of Divine grace are not to be considered as a blind impulse: but God's Spirit works on the spirit of man, as one rational being on another. The apostle therefore put the question with great reason, *How shall they believe in him, of whom they have not heard?* Rom. x. 14. And as some kuowledge is the foundation on which the Spirit of God ordinarily operates in men's hearts; so in proportion to the degree in which you attain further light into the scheme of the gospel, and of salvation by Christ, it may be expected you will be more impressed by it. The mention of this is so much the more necessary, as mistaken notions of religion often expose people on the one hand, to great perplexities, and on the other, betray them into a false peace, which one way or another *will be bitterness in the end.*

Come, therefore, to the house of God, and attend spiritual preaching. The question is not about forms, but things. Be not therefore overscrupulous about what is merely circumstantial in religion, on the one hand or the other: but where you find more spiritual light and improvement, there choose generally to attend: not confining religion to any particular party, nor judging those who differ from you in their sentiment or practice; but calmly and humbly seeking your own edification, leaving others to seek theirs where they are persuaded, in the sight of God, they may most probably find it.

Above all, remember, in this circumstance, to make *the word of God the man of your counsel,* (Psal. cxix. 24,) and to judge of what you read and hear by the tenor of that, as the oracle of eternal truth; always attending the reading of it with earnest prayer to God for the illumination of his Spirit, as I shall afterwards more particularly direct. No other books are to be set up in opposition to this, or in comparison with it; yet let it be your care, in subordination to scripture, to study the writings of those faithful servants of God in latter ages, who themselves manifest a sense of practical religion. Especially endeavor to find out and peruse those writings which treat of conversion and regeneration, and which contain advice suited to your case. Blessed be God, our language abounds with such: and every truly Christian minister will be glad to direct you to them, and so far as he has a convenient opportunity to furnish you with them.

4. Pour out your soul before God in earnest prayer.

You cannot be unacquainted with the many promises God has made in scripture for the encouragement of those who desire to pray to him in the sincerity of their hearts. You know into how little a compass Christ has crowded together three equivalent promises. *Ask, and it shall be given you: seek and ye shall find: knock, and it shall be opened unto you;* (Matt. vii. 7;) and you cannot but remember the threefold encouragement, from the success of those who have recourse to this expedient, which he has added in the most express and general terms: *For every one that asketh, receiveth; and he that seeketh, findeth; and to him that knocketh, it shall be opened.*

Verse 8. Go, therefore, in a cheerful dependence upon this promise: go, and try the truth of it. Whither should a creature in such circumstances go, but to that God, who has *the hearts* of all *in his hand as the rivers of water, and turns them whithersoever he will?* Prov. xxi. 1. And who should go to him, rather than you? And in what circumstances should a distressed creature rather think of looking and crying to him, than in these; where it sees itself surrounded with so much danger, and yet feels an inward earnest desire, not only of deliverance, but of holiness, too? Go, therefore, and cast yourself at the feet of God this very evening: do it as soon as you return to your habitations; and if you can not put your thoughts and desires into words, at least sigh and groan before the Lord. Mourn, if you can not pray; and mourn that you can not; or rather be assured, that unutterable groanings have sometimes the greatest efficacy, and prove the most prevailing eloquence.

It will be no wonder at all, if in these circumstances Satan should endeavor to terrify you. It is his common practice. So many souls have vanquished him upon their knees, that he dreads and hates the posture: but draw an argument from that very opposition to make you so much the more eager and importunate; and *when your heart is overwhelmed within you*, fly *unto the rock that is higher than you.* Psal. lxi. 2.

I will add, Be not discouraged, though help be not immediately imparted. Though you may seem to be *cast out of* God's *sight*, yet *look again towards his holy temple:* (Jonah ii. 4:) though you may seem to *cry from the deep*, and almost *from the belly of hell*, (Ver. 2,) the bowels of a heavenly Father will yearn over you as returning prodigals; and I doubt not you will meet with the reception that Ephraim found, when God saw him *bemoaning* and humbling *himself*, because he had been *as a bullock unaccustomed to the yoke:* when he cried, *Turn thou me, and I shall be turned: for thou art the Lord my God;* his heavenly Father answers him in these most affectionate words: attend to them, O thou returning sinner, for thy comfort in this hour of distress! *Is Ephraim my dear son? is he a pleasant child? for since I spake against him, I do earnestly remember him still; therefore my bowels are troubled for him, and I will surely have mercy upon him, saith the Lord.* Jer. xxxi. 18, 20.

5. I would advise you farther, that you immediately communicate the state of your case to some experienced Christian.

I know there is a backwardness in persons of your circumstances to do it; and it has been surprising to me to learn from some, who, in this respect, have afterwards grown wiser, how long they have been pining away in their sorrows before they could be persuaded to consult their ministers or Christian friends. It is a stratagem of Satan, against which I would by all means caution you. And one would think your own reason should suggest some very obvious advantages attending the method I propose, of opening your case freely to those whom you think to be more experienced in these things. The impression may be revived upon your own souls, even by the account you give them: and their advice may be exceeding useful to you to guard you against the wiles of the enemy which they have known, though hitherto you have been strangers to them; and to guide you into such methods as, by the Divine blessing, may farther promote that good work which seems, in any measure, to have been begun within you. You may also depend upon it that it will engage their prayers for you; which, in this case, may have great prevalency. And it will also naturally lead them to inspect your conduct: and if they see you afterwards in danger of being drawn aside, they may remind you of the hopes once entertained, and the impressions once made upon your mind. In this respect you may hope, that by *walking with wise men* you *will be yet wiser;* (Prov. xiii. 20;) and will soon find how happy an exchange you make, when you give up your vain, and perhaps wicked companions, that you may become *the companion of them that fear God, and that keep his precepts;* (Psal. cxix. 63;) and may have *your delight in them,* who, in the judgment of God, are *the excellent of the earth,* (Psal. xvi. 3,) however they may be despised and derided by men.

6. I would also advise that you endeavor to search out those, if there be any such about or near you, who are much in your own circumstances.

Observe, especially among young people, whether there are any that seem of late to have grown more serious than ordinary; and particularly more constant in attending the ordinances of God, and more cautious in venturing on occasions and temptations to sin; and if you can discover such, endeavor to form an acquaintance with them. Try by proper hints how far their circumstances resemble yours; and as you find encouragement, enter into a stricter friendship with them, founded on religion, and intended to promote it in each other's hearts. Associate yourselves in little bands for Christian converse and prayer; and by this means you will quicken and strengthen the hearts of each other. For on the one hand, what they tell you of their own experience will much confirm you in a persuasion that what you find in yourselves is not a mere fancy, but is really *a Divine work* begun on your hearts, and will give you encouragement to pursue it as such; for *as face answers to face, in water, so does the heart of man to man.* Prov. xxvii. 19. And on the other hand, the observation of your pious zeal will quicken others, and may occasion the revival of religion in the hearts of older Christians; as I bless God, I have found some things of this kind have done, and hope, and through the Divine blessing expect, to find it more and more. Therefore *exhort one another daily, while it is called to-day, lest any of you should be hardened through the deceitfulness of sin.* Heb. iii. 13. *Strengthen ye the weak hands and confirm the feeble knees;* (Isa. xxxv. 3;) and be assured, that while you are endeavoring to help others, you will find in yourselves the first fruits of this happy attempt; and while you *water others,* you *will be watered also yourselves.*

7. It is an advice of the highest importance, that whoever you are, you should *immediately fly to Christ,* and repose the confidence of your souls upon him.

Observe that I urge you, WHOEVER YOU ARE, to

fly immediately to Christ: and this I do, to guard against a strange notion which some are ready to entertain, as if we were to bring something of our own righteousness and obedience to him, to render us worthy of being accepted by him. But this is a grand mistake. The blessings of the gospel are not to be considered as matter of bargain and sale: no, if we *come to buy wine and milk*, it must be *without money and without price;* (Isa. lv. 1;) and *whoever will take of the water of life*, must do it *freely*. Rev. xxii. 17. If he pretend to offer an equivalent, he forfeits his share in the invitation; and must be made to know, that the price he offers is a great affront to the value of the blessings for which he would thus barter.

Let this then be your language, "Lord, I have undone myself, and in me is no help; I see nothing in myself which makes me worthy of thy regard; but this I know, that *where sin has abounded, grace does much more abound, and reigns through righteousness unto eternal life by Jesus Christ;* (Rom. v. 20, 21;) *through whom* thou hast assured me in thy word that *eternal life is the gift of God.* Rom. vi. 23. As such let me receive it: and by how much the more undeserving I have been, by so much the more will I celebrate the riches of thy grace in making me a vessel of mercy, and a monument of love throughout all eternity. Blessed Jesus, thou hast said, that *him who comes unto thee thou wilt in no wise cast out;* (John vi. 37;) behold, I come, and cast myself at thy feet; receive me, and *put me among the children,* (Jer. iii. 19,) though I deserve not the very *crumbs that fall from thy table.*" Matt. xv. 27.

You will not, I hope, imagine that when I give such advice as this, I mean to insinuate that a person, purposing to continue in his sins, may nevertheless come and receive the blessings of the gospel: for that would be no other than in the grossest manner to pervert and contradict the whole tenor of it. But this I say, and repeat it, that when once a sinner finds himself, by Divine grace, disposed to turn from his sins to God, and made willing to accept the mercy tendered in the gospel, of which a deliverance from sin and a renovation of nature are a great, important, and essential part; he may with cheerfulness apply himself to the great Redeemer, as one of those whom he came on purpose to deliver; and in proportion to the degree in which he can discern the sincerity of his sentiments, he may open his heart to comfort, how great soever his former unworthiness has been, and how lately soever such impressions may have been made upon his heart.

8. Make the dedication of yourselves to Christ and his service as solemn a thing as you can.

We read in the Acts of some that *were baptized*, and publicly *received into the church* the very *same day* in which they *were converted.* Acts ii. 41, 47. Though a change of circumstances may at present render it convenient to defer doing it for some time, because it is proper that the efficacy of your repentance and conversion should first of all be so far seen, as in the judgment of charity to approve the sincerity of it: yet I think, when you feel your hearts absolutely determined for God, you should in a solemn manner lay hold of his covenant, in secret at least, as soon as possible; and declare, as before him that searcheth all hearts, the sincerity of that acceptance. Some have recommended the doing this in a written engagement: and there are several very affecting forms of this kind in books on this subject, which may very profitably be used. But I hope the fullness of your heart will dictate something of this kind, if such helps should be wanting, or if any peculiar consideration should prevent their being used.

And surely, if you feel the love of the blessed Jesus glowing in your hearts as you ought, you will need no other engagement to yield yourselves to him: that love will be instead of ten thousand arguments; and you will see a secret charm in the view of serving him, which will engage your very soul to spring forward with vigor and eagerness to every proper instance of it. The dread of future punishment has certainly its use to restrain from the commission of sin, especially in an hour of pressing temptation; and the hope of that *exceeding and eternal weight of glory*, which the gospel promises, will have a still greater efficacy upon a generous mind: yet I will venture to say, that a heart powerfully impressed with the love of Jesus will have a stronger influence than either of these. Cordial friendship needs not to be hired to perform its proper office. Love is a law to itself: it adds a delightful relish to every attempt for the service of its object: and it is most evidently thus in the present case.

"Lord," will the Christian say, "wilt thou do me the honor to accept any feeble attempt for thy service which I can form? I thank thee for it, and bow my head before thee in the most grateful acknowledgments, that thou favorest me with an ability to discharge, in any degree, the fullness of my grateful heart in presenting them. O that my whole soul might daily rise before thee as an acceptable sacrifice in the flame of love! O that

I might always feel *my heart enlarged, to run the way of thy commandments!* Psal. cxix. 32. Were the degree of my future happiness from this moment invariably fixed, I would still pursue this delightful business; for there is no other in which my soul could find a pleasure equal, or comparable to it." If you feel such thoughts as these rising in your mind, breathe them out before the throne from day to day; and when you have done it, recollect frequently *the vows of God* that are *upon you;* (Psal. lvi. 12;) and see, that *having sworn, you perform it,* (Ps. cxix. 106,) and maintain in the whole of your lives a conduct agreeable to such a profession as this.

9. Gird up the loins of your mind to encounter a great deal of difficulty in your Christian course.

Many are the difficulties that you must expect; great, and possibly for a while increasing difficulties. It is commonly said, indeed, that those difficulties which attend the entrance on a religious life are the greatest; and in themselves considered, no doubt but they are so: they arise from many quarters, and unite all together in the same design of keeping you from a believing application to Christ, and a resolute closure with him. In this respect, evil sometimes arises to a man *in his own house;* (Matt. x. 35, 36;) and those, whose near relation should rather engage them to give the young convert the best assistanee where his most important interests are concerned, are on the contrary ready to lay a stumbling block in his way; and perhaps act as if they had rather he should have no religion at all, than change a few circumstances in the outward profession of it. Worldly interest, too, is perhaps to be sacrificed; and conscience cannot be preserved without giving up the friendship of those whom at any other expense but conscience a man would gladly oblige. And it is no wonder if Satan make his utmost efforts, and those very unwearied, too, that he may prevent the revolt of these subjects, or rather the escape of his prisoners. The Christian is therefore called upon by the apostle to arm himself as for a combat, and that at all points; to *put on the whole armor of God, that he may be able to withstand in the evil day; and having done all, to stand.* Ephes. vi. 11, 13.

Nor must you, my friends, though as soon as you have *put on your harness* you gain some important victory, *boast* as if you might securely *put it off.* 1 Kings xx. 11. Your whole life must be a series of exercise. *Through* much opposition, as well as *much tribulation, you must enter into the kingdom of God:* (Luke ix. 62:) and though your difficulties may generally be greatest at first, yet your encouragements then may perhaps be so peculiarly great, and your spirits under their first religious impressions so warm, that other difficulties, in themselves smaller, may afterwards press more sensibly upon you. Endeavor therefore to keep yourselves in a prepared posture. Put on a steady resolution; and to support it, *sit down and count the cost, lest having begun to build,* you shamefully desist and *be not able to finish it;* (Luke xiv. 28, 30;) or *lest having put your hand to the plow,* you should *look back,* and become *unfit for the kingdom of God.* Luke ix. 62. And therefore,

10. Let every step in this attempt be taken with a deep sense of your own weakness, and on humble dependence upon Divine grace to be communicated to you as the matter requires.

Recollect seriously what I was telling you in a former discourse, of the necessity of a Divine agency and interposition; and remember, it depends upon God, not only to *begin the good work,* but also to carry it on, and *perform it until the day of Jesus Christ.* Phil. i. 6. If we *trust in our hearts,* especially after this solemn admonition, this plain instruction, added to such frequent experience, we *are fools* indeed. Prov. xxviii. 26. Let us therefore *trust in the Lord, and not lean to our own understanding.* Prov. iii. 5. And do you, my friends, who have but just enlisted yourselves in this holy war, every one of you say, with an humble yet cheerful heart, *in the name of our God will we set up our banners.* Psal. xx. 5. And if thus you *wait on the Lord,* you *shall renew your strength*; and even the *feeblest soul* shall be enabled by *Divine grace* to *mount up with wings as eagles,* and to press on from one degree of religious improvement to another, while *the youths shall faint and be weary, and the young men shall utterly fall.* Isa. xl. 30, 31. The Apostle expresses, in the liveliest manner, his dependence on the Divine Redeemer to communicate this grace in a proper degree, when he says, *Let us come boldly to the throne of grace, that we may obtain mercy, and find grace to help in time of need:* (Heb. iv. 16:) plainly implying, that it may be obtained if we have but hearts to seek for it; which, as on the one hand, it effectually takes off all idle excuses for the neglect of our duty, pleaded from our own acknowledged weakness, any further than we are supported by Divine power; so on the other hand it animates the heart, that, sensible of its various infirmities, desires nevertheless to go forth to the work of God, and to consecrate all its faculties to his service; using them, such as they are, for God, and humbly seeking from him the enlargement of them.

Go, therefore, my friends, into the Divine presence; and while under a sense of this be not discouraged, though mountains of opposition may lie in your way. Those *mountains shall be made low*, and spread themselves into *a plain* before you; (Isa. xi. 4;) while you go forth under the influences of the Spirit of the Lord who *is able to make all grace abound* to his people. 2 Cor. ix. 8. Of this Paul in our text was a most celebrated instance, who not only *received*, as was here promised, *directions what he should do*, but had strength also given him to perform it; a *strength*, which was *made perfect* and illustrious in his *weakness:* (2 Cor. xii. 9:) and when, in consequence of this, he had attained to very distinguished improvements in religion, and had been enabled to act up, in the most honorable manner, not only to the Christian character in general, but to that of a minister and an apostle, he acknowledges, in all his *abundant labors*, that it was not *he, but the grace of God that was with him.* 1 Cor. xv. 10.

If he be thus with you, my dear friends, you will be *established and built up in your most holy faith.* Col. ii. 7; Jude ver. 20. The most agreeable hopes we form concerning you, when we see you under such serious impressions as this discourse supposes, will be answered; and they *who have spoken to you the word of God,* on such occasions as these, will have the pleasure to think that they *have not run in vain.* Phil. ii. 16.

And now if these directions, which I have offered to you with great plainness and freedom, but with the sincerest desire of your edification and establishment in religion, be seriously pursued, I shall have the satisfaction of thinking, that though I might find you in the number of the unregenerate when I began these lectures, I shall carry you on along with me in a new character through the only head that yet remains to be handled. I shall indeed address myself to you, as those who *were sometimes darkness, but are now light in the Lord,* (Eph. v. 8,) when I proceed to address those who have been renewed by Divine grace; which I promised as my last general topic, and with which I shall conclude my discourses on this important subject.

DISCOURSE X.

AN ADDRESS TO THE REGENERATE, FOUNDED ON THE PRECEDING DISCOURSES.

JAMES I. 18.

Of his own will begat he us with the word of truth, that we should be a kind of first fruits of his creatures.

I INTEND the words which I have now been reading, only as an introduction to that *address to the sons and daughters of the Lord Almighty,* with which I am now to conclude these lectures; and therefore shall not enter into any critical discussion, either of them, or of the context.

I hope God has made the series of these discourses, in some measure, useful to those for whose service they were immediately intended: but if they have not been so to all, and if with relation to many I have *labored in vain* from Sabbath to Sabbath, I cannot be surprised at it. *What am I better than my fathers?* 1 Kings xix. 4. It has, in every age, been their complaint, that they *have stretched out their hands all the day to a disobedient and gainsaying people;* (Isa. lxv. 2: Rom. x. 21;) that *the bellows* have been *burnt,* and *the lead consumed of the fire,* but the dross has *not been taken away:* such *reprobate silver* have multitudes been found. Jer. vi. 29, 30. Yea, the Lord Jesus Christ himself, who spake with such unequaled eloquence, with such divine energy, yet met with multitudes, who were *like the deaf adder,* that *would not hearken to the voice of the* wisest *charmer:* (Ps. lviii. 4, 5:) and surely *the disciple is not above his master, nor the servant above his lord.* Matt. x. 24.

When indeed we consider the infinite importance of the message we address to you, O ye perishing sinners! we hardly know how to give over, or to take a denial. We feel a strong impulse on our hearts to give *line upon line,* and *precept upon precept:* (Isa. xxviii. 10:) as a physician that loves his patient, when he sees the distemper prevailing, and has run through the whole range of medicines, is ready, while life yet remains, not entirely to give over, but to repeat again what he had prescribed unsuccessfully before. And if God spares our lives, no doubt many of those things which I have before been urging, must in substance be repeated. But at present I will desist: I know not what more or further to say; and if you are utterly unimpressed with what I have already laid before you, especially with regard to the character of the unregenerate—the nature of regeneration—the absolute necessity of it—and of the Divine agency in producing it, with the absolute importance of your securing a part in the kingdom of heaven ; I know not what further to urge, and must leave you either to the grace or the judgment of God.

The time will certainly come, when you will see and own the importance of these things. The word of God will, in one sense or another, take hold of every soul that hears it, and, perhaps on some of you in a very terrible manner, and in a very little time. But if it do, I may say with the apostle Paul, when in token of the solemnity with which he spoke, *he shook his raiment*, and took leave of his obstinate hearers, *I am clean from your blood;* (Acts xviii. 6 ;) and since you refuse to be instructed, I turn to those who regard what I say. And thus, according to the method I at first proposed, I proceed,

Seventhly, To conclude these discourses with an address to those who, by Divine grace, are experimentally acquainted with this great work of regeneration ; to show them how they ought to be affected with the consideration of the truths that have been offered, and what improvement they should make of such a course of sermons as you have lately been attending.

Out of a general regard to the glory of God and the good of souls, you have attended on what has hitherto been spoken to persons of a very different character; and I hope not altogether without some sensible refreshment and advantage; but now hear more immediately for yourselves, and *suffer a word of exhortation* in such particulars as these: Be thankful to God for what you have experienced; improve it as an engagement to behave in a suitable manner; study to promote the work of God upon the hearts of others; and long for that blessed world where the change that is now begun, and is gradually advancing in your souls, shall be universal and complete. Your own wisdom and piety have, no doubt, anticipated me in each of these particulars; but you will be glad to enter more fully into the reflection than you could do, while it was intermingling itself with other thoughts.

I. Return the most affectionate acknowledgments of praise to the God of all mercy for the experience you have had of a regenerating change.

I would now address this exhortation and charge to every one of you, who, through Divine grace, hope you can say, that you are *born again;*

to all who can say, that God *has, of his own will, begotten you with the word of truth, that you may be a kind of first fruits of his creatures.* To you I would say, *Sing unto the Lord, O ye saints of his, and give thanks at the remembrance of his holiness* and goodness. Psal. xxx. 4. *Give thanks to the Father, who has made you meet to be partakers of the inheritance of the saints in light.* Col. i. 12. Join your voices and your hearts in the most cheerful hymns of praise, whatever your different circumstances are. Let the young and the old, the rich and the poor, the honorable and the mean, rejoice together; if any may be called poor, who are thus enriched; if any may be accounted mean, who are thus honored. *Bless the Lord at all times,* let *his praise be continually in your mouths;* (Ps. xxxiv. 1;) and endeavor to carry along with you, through the darkest road you travel, and the bitterest sorrows you taste, cheerfulness in your hearts, and praise on your tongues; considering—how important the blessing is with which the Lord has favored you; how few there are who partake of it; and in the midst of how much opposition the Divine grace has taken hold of your souls, and wrought its wonders of love there.

1. Consider, my Christian friends, how important this favor is which God has bestowed upon

you, in thus *begetting you as a kind of first fruits of his creatures.*

Justly indeed may we say, *Behold what manner of love the Father hath bestowed upon us,* that *we should* be regenerated by his grace, and so *be called,* and that with propriety, *the sons of God!* 1 John iii. 1. Justly may I say to you, now you are assembled in the *courts of the Lord,* in those emphatical words of David, *O come, let us worship, and bow down; let us kneel before the Lord our Maker;* (Psal. xcv. 6;) for *it is he that has made us and not we ourselves,* with regard to this second, as well as the first creation; and *we,* in consequence of it, *are* in the noblest sense, *his people, and the sheep of his pasture: enter,* therefore, *into his gates with thanksgiving, and into his courts with praise; be thankful unto him, and bless his name.* Ps. c. 3, 4.

My brethren, it is a favor in which the salvation of your souls is concerned; and can that be small? or ought it ever to be thought of but with the highest emotion and enlargedness of heart? The gracious purposes of God towards his children are to make every one of them *higher than the kings of the earth,* (Psal. lxxxix. 27,) to give them more solid satisfaction than crowns and kingdoms can afford, and at length to raise them to a diadem of immortal glory. Oh what reason have you with the Apostle, to say, *Blessed be the God and Father of our Lord Jesus Christ, who, according to his abundant mercy, has begotten us again to a lively hope, by the resurrection of Jesus Christ from the dead,* even to the hope of *an inheritance incorruptible and undefiled, and that fadeth not away, reserved in heaven for us, who are kept by the power of God through faith unto salvation!* 1 Pet. i. 3–5. Survey this great privilege which God has already given you, this high security, these glorious hopes. Has he not brought the beginning of glory already into your souls? Has he not wrought you to a filial temper, and taught you to cry, *Abba, Father?* Gal. iv. 6. Has he not, in some measure, formed and fashioned your minds to a meetness to dwell with angels and perfected spirits in heaven? So that you can now say, even with relation to that which you already feel, that *you are no more strangers and foreigners, but fellow-citizens with the saints, and of the household of God.* Eph. ii. 19. You are even *now the sons of God, and it doth not yet appear what you shall be;* (1 John iii. 2;) but there is enough appears, and enough known at present, of what you are, and what you shall be, to revive, to delight, to transport the heart.

And is not this too, O thou afflicted soul, who art called to encounter the most painful difficulties, enough to be the means of thy support, and to afford thee matter for thy strong consolation? You that are *tossed with tempests*, (Isa. liv. 11,) and obliged to struggle under various and long continued burdens, have you not here a joy that the world can neither bestow nor impair, a pleasure in public and in secret duties, and *a hope*, which is *as the anchor of the soul both sure and steadfast, entering into that within the vail*, (Heb. vi. 19,) and so enabling you to outride these storms and tempests? How glorious does your lot appear when viewed in the light of scripture! You are expressly told, *All things are yours:* (1 Cor. iii. 21:) *the Lord will give grace and glory, and no good thing will he withhold from* you: (Psal. lxxxiv. 11:) *all the paths of the Lord are mercy and truth to* you; (Psal. xxv. 10;) and ere long you shall see how they are so. You have a sight by faith of the inheritance appointed for his children; but he does not intend merely a distant prospect for you: *you shall go in and possess that good land*, (Deut. iv. 22,) and shall ere long *be absent from the body, and present with the Lord:* (2 Cor. v. 8:) yea, *the Lord Jesus Christ*, ere long, *shall come to be glorified in his saints, and to be admired in all them that believe*, (2 Thess. i. 10,) to be glorified and admired, in and by you in particular; when bearing the image of your heavenly

Father, you shall rise far beyond this earth and all its vain anxieties, and vainer amusements, to dwell forever in his presence. And what is there in this world that you imagine you want, which is by any means to be compared with these enjoyments and hopes? Surely, sirs, in such a view, you should be much more than content; and should feel your inward admiration, love, and joy, bursting the bonds of silence, and turning your voices, that have been broken by sighs, into the most cheerful and exalted anthems of praise: especially when you consider,

2. How few there are who partake of this important favor, which God has extended to you.

I hope I need not, after all I have said, remind you at large, that I intend not by any means to speak, as excluding those of different forms and different experiences; as if, in consequence of that diversity, they had *neither part nor lot in this matter.* Acts viii. 21. I hope that many who are not so ready, as it were to be wished, to *receive one another,* are nevertheless, in this respect, *received by Christ to the glory of God.* Rom. xv. 7. Yet the temper and conduct of the generality of mankind, even under a Christian profession, too plainly show, that they have the marks of eternal ruin upon them: and one can form no hope concerning them, consistent with the tenor of the whole word of God, any other than this, that possibly they may hereafter be changed into something contrary to what they are, and in that change be happy.

Now that you are not left among the wide extended ruins of mankind, but are set as pillars in the building of God, is what you have been taught by the preceding discourses to refer to the grace of God, which has taken and polished you to the form you now bear. Or, as the Evangelist expresses it, in language more suitable to the subject before us, *the power*, or privilege, *to become the sons of God*, is what *he gives to as many as receive him;* and it is manifest as to your regeneration, that *you are born, not of blood, nor of the will of the flesh, nor of the will of man, but of God:* (John i. 12, 13:) for *we love him, because he first loved us;* (1 John iv. 12;) and whatsoever our attainments be, there is no true believer but will be ready, with the Apostle Paul, to say, *By the grace of God I am what I am.* 1 Cor. xv. 10.

And now, when these two thoughts are taken in this comparison with each other, how deeply should they impress our minds! And how should it excite us to the most lively gratitude, to consider that when so many of our fellow-creatures perish, even under the sound of the gospel; that when they live and die under the power of a corrupt and degenerate nature, despising all the means which God has given them of becoming better, and turning them into the occasion of greater mischief; God should graciously incline our hearts to a wiser and better choice! It is indeed a melancholy reflection, that the number of those who are made *wise to salvation* should be so small; yet it is an endearing circumstance in the Divine goodness to us, that when it is so small, we should be included in it: as no doubt it would appear to every truly religious person in the ark, that when but *eight souls were saved* from the deluge, he should be one. *There is now a remnant*, says the Apostle, *according to the election of grace:* (Rom. xi. 5:) to that grace therefore should we render the praise. We have indeed chosen him; but it is in consequence of *his choosing us.* John xv. 16. We have said, *The Lord is my portion;* but let us remember to *bless him* that *he has given us* that *counsel*, (Psal. xvi. 5, 7,) in consequence of which we have been inclined to do it. Again,

3. Consider, in the midst of how much opposition the grace of God has laid hold on your souls, and wrought its wonders of love there.

Christians, look into your own hearts; yea, look back upon your own lives, and see whether many of you have not reason to say, with the great Apostle, *It is a faithful saying, and worthy of all acceptation, that Christ Jesus came into the world to save sinners, of whom I am chief:* (1 Tim. i. 15:) and yet *to me, who am less than the least of all saints, is this given,* (Eph. iii. 8,) that I should be a regenerate, adopted child of God, begotten to an inheritance of eternal glory.

"Oh," may one Christian say, "how obstinately did I strive against my own happiness! like a poor creature that, having received some dangerous wound, and being delirious with a fever attending it, struggles with the hand that is stretched out to heal him. How did I draw back from the yoke of God! How did I trifle with convictions, and put them off from one time to another! So that God might most righteously have awakened any heart rather than mine. He admonished me by his word, and by his providence; he sent afflictions; he wrought out deliverances for me; and yet I went on to harden my heart, as if I had been afflicted and delivered, that I might work greater *abominations;* (Jer. vii. 10;) till *the Lord being merciful to me, laid hold upon me, and drew me out of Sodom.*" Gen. xx. 16.

And here another Christian will be ready to say within himself, "If the grace of God wrought sooner upon me, when my soul was more pliant, when my heart was comparatively tender in infancy or childhood, or in early youth; yet what ungrateful returns have I since made for his mercy! How defective have I been in those fruits of holiness which might reasonably have been expected from me, who have so long a time been *planted in the house of the Lord!* Alas for me! that I have *flourished* no more *in the courts of my God.* Psal. xcii. 13. How often have I forgotten and forsaken him; how cold and negligent has my spirit been, how inconstant my walk, how indolent my behavior, for these many years that have passed since I was first brought into his family! How little have I done in his service in proportion to the advantages I have enjoyed! All this he foresaw; all the instances in which my *goodness* would be *as a morning cloud, and as the early dew;* (Hos. vi. 4;) all the instances in which this perverse heart of mine, so prone to backslide, should *turn aside,* and start back from him *like a deceitful bow:* (Psal. lxxviii. 57:) and yet he has mercy upon me, I know not why. I cannot pretend to account for it any otherwise than by saying, *Even so, Father, for so it seemed good in thy sight:* (Matt. xi. 26:) *thou hast mercy on whom thou wilt have mercy, and thou hast compassion on whom thou wilt have compassion.* Rom. ix. 15. I have revolted deeply from thee again and again; yet thou sufferest me not to be lost to this very day, nor wilt thou ever suffer it: *Thou restorest my soul; thou leadest me in the paths of righteousness for thy name's sake.* Psal. xxiii. 3. *Having therefore obtained help from God, I continue to this day*; (Acts xxvi. 2;) and *surely goodness and mercy shall follow me all the days of my life;* and unworthy as I am so much as to enter into thine house below, *I shall dwell in the house of the Lord forever* above. Psal. xxiii. 6. Thus, Lord, thou makest me, as it were, a wonder to myself; and I hope to express my admiration and my gratitude throughout eternal ages: and if I can vie with the rest of thy redeemed ones in nothing else, I will at least do it in bowing low before thy throne, and acknowledging that I am of the number of the most unworthy, in whom my Lord has been pleased to glorify the riches of his mercy, and the freedom of his grace."

In the mean time, Christians, I call you often to entertain yourselves with such views as these, often to excite your hearts by such lively considerations; I call you, in the name of your Father and your Saviour, to a whole life of gratitude and praise. And this leads me to add,

II. Improve those experiences you have had of Divine grace, as an engagement to behave in a suitable manner.

Remember the lively admonition of the text,

that you were *begotten by him* for this very purpose, *that you should be a kind of first-fruits of his creatures.* See, therefore, that ye be entirely consecrated to him; and behave as becomes the *children of God, in the midst of a crooked and perverse generation:* being not only *harmless and blameless* among them, *but shining as lights in the world, and holding forth* that *word of life*, (Phil. ii. 16,) by which he has begotten you to himself, *and quickened you when you were dead in trespasses and sins.* Eph. ii. 1, 5.

God has now brought you into a most honorable relation: he may therefore well expect more, much more from you than from others. He has *made you as his children, kings and priests to himself*, (Rev. i. 6,) and you are therefore to *offer up spiritual sacrifice, acceptable to God by Jesus Christ.* 1 Pet. ii. 5. *You were once darkness, but now are ye light in the Lord; walk*, therefore, *as children of light.* Eph. v. 8. Remember *you are not your own;* (1 Cor. vi. 19;) your time, your possessions, and all your capacities for service, are the property of your heavenly Father. And permit me to remind you, that if you desire to see this doctrine of regeneration prevail, you, who profess to be experimentally acquainted with it, must take great care that your behavior may not only be innocent, but exemplary: otherwise many will be ready to *blaspheme the holy name* of that *God*, (2 Sam. xii. 14,) whom you call your Father; and you are like to bring a reproach upon the *household of faith*, which probably you will never be able to roll away.

Christians, the dignity of our birth and our hopes is too little considered and regarded; and the reason why the world thinks so meanly of it, is because we ourselves are so insensible of its excellency. Did we apprehend it more, we should surely be more solicitous to *walk worthy of* that *calling wherewith we are called*, (Eph. iv. 1,) that high and holy calling. Let me, therefore, exhort you to endeavor to loosen your affections more from these entanglements of time and sense, which so much debase our minds, and dishonor our lives. *Yield yourselves unto God as those that are alive from the dead:* (Rom. vi. 13:) employ, with a growing zeal, to the honor of God, that renewed life which he has given you: *Be not conformed to this world, but be ye transformed by the renewing of your minds:* (Rom. xii. 2:) and let your conversation and behavior be like those who *feel* the *constraining influences of Divine love*, (2 Cor. v. 14;) who are, not in form, but in reality, devoted to God; and who would be continually *waiting for his salvation*, (Gen. xlix. 18,) with that temper in which you could most desire that salvation to find you when it comes.

III. Let those who have experienced the power of Divine grace themselves, study to promote the work of God upon the hearts of others.

Labor, as much as possible, to spread this temper which God has wrought in your hearts; for you cannot but know that with it you spread true happiness, which alone is to be found in that intercourse with the great Author of our being, for which this lays the foundation, and in the regular exercise of those powers which are thus sanctified. No sooner was Paul converted himself, but he presently set himself to bring others to Christ, and to *preach the faith which once he destroyed.* Gal. i. 13. And David speaks of it as the effects of God's pardoning love to him, *Then will I teach transgressors thy ways, and sinners shall be converted unto thee.* Psal. li. 13.

If, therefore, God has called us to the office of the ministry, as the experience of this change on our own hearts will be our best qualification for our public work, and indeed such a qualification that nothing else can supply the want of it; so it will surely excite us in a very powerful manner to apply vigorously to this care. *That which we have* not only *heard*, but *seen with our eyes, and looked upon, and handled of the word of life,* let us *declare to others; that their fellowship also may be with the Father, and with his Son Jesus Christ.* 1 John i. 1, 3. Let us declare it in our public discourses, and never be ashamed to bear our testimony to that grace to which we are so much indebted; to *that grace by which we are what we are.* 1 Cor. xv. 10. Let us *warn every man, and teach every man* the absolute necessity of regeneration; and expose the vanity of all those hopes which are built upon any fair outside, on any moral decency of behavior, or any humane turn of temper, on any warm flight of imagination or emotion of the passions, while the soul continues unrenewed and unsanctified. Let us endeavor to *save men with fear, pulling them out of the fire,* (Jude ver. 23,) which, if they are yet unregenerate, is just ready to kindle upon them. And let us be often reviewing our respective flocks, that we may see who they are, concerning whom there is reason to entertain this fear; that proper applications may be made to them in private, as well as in public; that joining our admonitions to our sermons, and our prayers and examples to both, we may at least *deliver our own souls,* (Ez. xxxiii. 9,) if we cannot deliver theirs. But in proportion to the degree that such a spirit prevails in us, there is very great encouragement to hope it will be propagated to them, and that *our labor shall not be in vain in the Lord.* 1 Cor. xv. 58.

And let me beseech you, my beloved hearers in other stations of life, that you would not imagine the work is so entirely ours that you have nothing to do with it. Are we alone redeemed by the blood of the Son of God? Are we alone renewed and sanctified by his grace? Are we alone the brethren and friends of mankind, that the generous care and endeavor to promote their eternal happiness should be entirely devolved upon us? We wish so well to the world, and permit us to say, we wish so well to you, to your own religious consolation and establishment, to your comfortable account, to your eternal reward, that we can not but earnestly exhort you all, even as many as *have tasted that the Lord is gracious*, (1 Peter ii. 3,) that in this respect you join, not only as I trust you do, your prayers with ours, but that you also join your endeavors.

Let me particularly address this exhortation to those of you who bear any distinguished office in the society, to whom therefore its religious interests are dear by additional ties Let me address those of you whose age and experience, in the human and the divine life, give you something of a natural authority in your application, and command a distinguished regard. Look round about you and observe the state of religion in your neighborhood; and labor to the utmost to propagate, not so much this or that particular opinion or form of worship, but real vital Christianity in the world. Bear your testimony to it on all proper occasions: be not ashamed of it in your familiar discourse; and above all, labor to adorn it by your actions. And when you see any under serious impressions, as it is certain they will have a great deal discouraging and difficult to break through; and as the devil and his instruments, among whom I must necessarily reckon licentious company, will be doing their utmost to draw them back into *the snare of the fowler;* let me exhort and charge you to be as solicitous to save as others are to destroy. I know how many excuses our cowardly and indolent hearts are ready to find out upon such an occasion: but I think those words of Solomon are a sufficient answer to all, and I beg you would seriously revolve them; *If thou forbear to deliver them that are drawn unto death, and those that are ready to be slain: if thou sayest, Behold we knew it not; doth not he that pondereth the heart consider it? and he that keepeth thy soul,* thine, Oh Christian, with such peculiar and gracious care, *doth not he know it? and shall not he render to every man according to his works?* Prov. xxiv.

11, 12. He will assuredly remember, and will abundantly reward, every *work of faith, and* every labor *of love;* (1 Thes. i. 3;) and we are insensible of our own true interest, if we do not see how much it is concerned here.

Let me especially leave this exhortation with you who are parents and heads of families. And one would imagine there should need but little importunity in such a case as this: one would think your own hearts should speak to you, upon such an occasion, in very pathetic language. Look upon your dear children, to whom you have conveyed a nature which you know to be degenerate and corrupt; and be earnest in your prayers before God, and your endeavors with them, that it may be renewed. And take care that you do not in this sense *despise* the soul *of your man-servant, or of your maid-servant.* Job xxxi. 13. God has brought them under your care, it may be in those years of life in which, on the one hand, they are most capable of being instructed and seriously impressed; and in which, on the other hand, they are also most in danger of being corrupted. Perhaps their relation to you, and abode with you, is the most advantageous circumstance which may occur in their whole lives: see therefore that you seize it with a holy eagerness; and amidst all the charges you give them relating to your own business, neglect not that of *the one thing needful;* (Luke x. 42;) and labor heartily to bring them to the honor and happiness which is common to all God's servants, and peculiar to them alone.

Let me conclude this part of my address with entreating you all to express your concern for the souls of others, by your importunate prayers to God for them. Pray for the success of gospel ordinances: and for a blessing on the labors of all God's faithful servants throughout our whole land, of one or another denomination in religion. Yea, pray that throughout the whole world, God would *revive his work in the midst of the years;* (Hab. iii. 2;) that the religion of his Son, by which so many souls have been regenerated, refined and saved, may be universally propagated; and that all who are vigorously engaged in so important, though so self-denying a work, may find that *the hand of the Lord is with them,* and *multitudes believe and turn unto the Lord;* (Acts xi. 21;) so that *his sons may be brought from far, and his daughters from the ends of the earth;* (Isaiah xliii. 6;) that *the barren may rejoice, and she that did not travail with child, may break forth into singing, and cry aloud;* that *the children of* nations now *strangers to Christ, may be more than of those* that are already *espoused to him.* Isa. liv. 1; Gal. iv. 27. And then,

IV. Let all that are born again, long for that blessed world, where the work of God shall be completed, and we shall appear with a dignity and glory becoming his children.

As for *God, his work is perfect;* (Deut. xxxii. 4;) and the time, the happy time is approaching, when we shall know, and the whole world shall know, in another manner than we now do, what our heavenly Father has intended for us in begetting us to himself. Whatever our attainments here may be, *we know* at present but *in part:* (1 Cor. xiii. 9;) and with whatever integrity of soul we now walk before God, we are sanctified but in part: and hereupon we find, and must expect to find, *the flesh striving against the Spirit,* as well as *the Spirit against the flesh: so that,* in many respects, *we cannot do the things that we would.* Gal. v. 17. In proportion to the degree in which our nature is refined and brightened, we are more sensible of the evil of these corruptions that remain within us; so that though we are not, in a strict propriety of speech, *carnal and sold under sin,* but do *indeed delight in the law of God after the inward man,* (Rom. vii. 14, 22,) yet in the humility of our hearts we are often borrowing that pathetic complaint, *Oh, wretched man that I am! who shall deliver me from the body of this death?* Verse 24.

But let it be remembered, Christians, as the matter of your joy, that the struggle shall not be perpetual, that it shall not indeed be long. *Look up* with pleasure then, *and lift up your heads; for your redemption draweth nigh.* Luke xxi. 28. The time is approaching, *when that which is perfect shall come,* and *that which is in part shall be done away.* 1 Cor. xiii. 10. You are *now the children of GOD;* but *it does not appear* to every eye that you are so: *the world knows us not.* 1 John iii. 1, 2. Nor are we to wonder at it: for even *Christ our Lord* was once *unknown,* and appeared in so much meanness, and so much calamity, that an undiscerning and carnal eye could not have discovered who and what he was. But there is a day appointed for *the manifestation of the sons of* GOD, (Rom. viii. 19,) as the apostle Paul most happily expresses it; when he will manifest them to each other, and manifest them also to the whole world. They shall not always live thus at a distance from their Father's house, and under those dispensations of Providence that look so much like disregard and neglect; but he will take them home, and gather them to himself. Ere long, Christians, he will call these heaven-born spirits of yours, that are now aspiring towards him, to dwell in his immediate presence: he will *receive you to himself;* and you shall stand, where no sinner shall have a place, *in the congregation of the righteous,* (Ps. ii. 5,) and shall have *an inheritance among the saints in light,* the saints in holiness and glory.

O happy day! when dropping this body in the grave, we shall ascend pure and joyful spirits to that triumphant assembly, where there is not one vitiated affection, not one foolish thought to be found among the thousands and ten thousands of God's Israel! O blessed period of a regenerate state! Though all the schemes of the Divine love were to rest here, and these bodies were forever to be laid aside, and utterly to be lost in the grave; the rejoicing soul might say, "Lord, it is enough!" And it might be indeed enough for us; but it is not enough to answer the gracious purposes of God's paternal love. God will show, in the most conspicuous manner, what a family he has raised to himself among the children of men; and therefore he will assemble them all in their complete persons, and will do it with solemn pomp and magnificent parade. He will for this purpose send his own Son, *with all his holy angels,* (Matt. xxv. 31,) and will cause the bodies of millions of his children, that have long dwelt in the dust, to spring out of it, at once in forms of beauty and lustre, worthy their relation to him. This, therefore, is, with beautiful propriety, called by the apostle *the adoption, even the redemption of our body;* (Rom. viii. 23;) alluding to the public ceremony, with which adoptions among the ancients were solemnly confirmed and declared, after they had been more privately transacted between the parties immediately concerned.

O, Christians, how reasonable is it that our souls should be rising with a secret ardor towards this blessed hope, this glorious abode!—It is pleasant for the children of God to meet and converse with one another upon earth; so pleasant, that I wonder they do not more frequently form themselves into little societies, in which, under that character, they should join their discourses and their prayers. It is delightful to address those that, we trust, through grace are born of God. No discourses are more pleasant than those that suit them: and could we, that are the ministers of Christ, reasonably hope, that we had none but such to attend our labors, we should joyfully confine our discourses to such subjects. Yet while we are here, we see imperfections in others, we feel them yet more painfully in ourselves: and as there is no pure, unmixed society, no fellowship on earth that is completely holy and without blemish, so there is now no pure delight, no perfect pleasure to be met with here. Oh when shall I depart from this mixed society, and reach that state where all is good, all glorious: where I shall see my heavenly Father, and all my brethren in the Lord; and shall behold them all forever acting up to their character! All *giving thanks to the Father, who has made us meet to be partakers of the inheritance of the saints in light!* Col. i. 12. All forever blessing and serving the great Redeemer; and without one ungenerous action, one reflecting word, one suspicious thought, forever serving each other in love, rejoicing in each other's happiness, and with the most prudent and steadfast application forever studying and laboring to improve it!

With the most earnest desire that you, my dear brethren and friends, may at length attain to this state of perfection and glory; and with a cheerful expectation, through Divine grace, that I shall ere long meet many of you in it, I close this sermon, and these discourses: not without an humble hope, that when we arrive at this blessed world, these hours, which we have spent together in the house ef God, in attending them, will come into a pleasant remembrance; and that the God of all grace, to whose glory they are faithfully devoted, and to whose blessing they are humbly committed, will honor them as the means of increasing his family, as well as of feeding and quickening those who are already his regenerate children!—AMEN.

POSTSCRIPT.

MEANING OF THE WORD REGENERATION.

To what I have said in the conclusion of the first discourse concerning the proper import of the word REGENERATION, I beg leave to add the following remarks for the farther satisfaction of some worthy persons, who think it may be convenient to state the matter a little more particularly.

I ACKNOWLEDGE that many learned and pious divines have taught and contended, that REGENERATION does, in the strictest propriety of speech, signify BAPTISM—so that *no unbaptized person*, how well disposed soever, can properly be said to be *regenerated;* whereas that title may justly be given to *all who have been baptized*, how destitute soever they might have been of Christian faith and holiness when they received the ordinance, or how grossly soever they may since have forfeited the final blessings of a regenerate state. *Dr. Waterland* has stated this matter at large in his labored and ingenious treatise on the subject, which is the best I know on this side of the question. And though this would be a very improper place to enter on a critical examination of that piece, I will briefly touch on the *chief arguments* which he, or others in his sentiments, have urged in vindication of this favorite notion. So far as I can recollect, what they say is capable of being reduced to two heads;—that *Christian antiquity* uses the word in this sense;—and that there are passages of *Scripture* which authorize such an application of it.

As to the first of these, I readily own that the word has this sense in the generality of the Christian writers, from about the middle of the *second century*, though I think not so universally as some have concluded:* but I think it easy to account for such a use of it among them. For in the earliest ages of the church, persons were generally *baptized* as soon as they were *converted* to the cordial belief of *Christianity;* and therefore the

* *Clemens Alexandrinus*, so often, and to be sure reasonably, quoted on the other side, plainly uses the word for *a change of character by true repentance;* (*Strom. lib.* ii. *page* 425,) where, speaking of *a penitent harlot*, he says, "that being born again by conversion, or a change in her temper and behavior, she has the regeneration of life:" αναγεννηθεισα κατα την επιςροφην τȣ βιȣ παλιγγενεσιαν εχει ζωης.

time of their *conversion*, and that of their *baptism*, might naturally enough be spoken of as one : and as this was a period when they did, as it were, *come into a new world*, it is no wonder that *the action* by which they testified a change so lately made, should be put for *that change* itself. Just as *illumination* also among the ancients signifies *baptism:* not to intimate that the grand illumination of the mind was made by this rite, or at the time of it; for that would be supposing the person in darkness when he embraced the Gospel, and determined to be baptized: but because it was taken for granted, and that very justly in those days, that *every one savingly enlightened* would soon be *baptized*, that so he might be regularly joined to the society of *enlightened* or *regenerated persons*, that is, to the *Christian church:* which no doubt had the best right of any body of men in the world to that title, though in its purest state it contained some ignorant and wicked members.

In a word, a man by *baptism* solemnly *professed himself a Christian;* and as it was generally *the first overt act* by which his believing the Gospel could be publicly and generally known, and was also supposed to be very near the time of his inward conversion, they dated *his regeneration*, that is, *his happy change* (as that word used to signify even among the heathen*) from that time. We own therefore that these *ancient Christians* (of whom I always think and speak with great respect) had a very good excuse for this method of speaking: but whether they were perfectly accurate in this, and whether they did not recede from the scripture use of the word, may be matter of farther inquiry.

As to the arguments from *Scripture* in support of the interpretation I oppose, they are taken partly from *particular places;* but chiefly, as I apprehend, from *the general tenor of it*, in which *Christians* are spoken of as *regenerated.*

THE *particular texts* are *John* iii. 5, and *Tit.* iii. 5, on which much of the stress of this contro-

* It is well known that *Cicero* expresses *the happy change* made in his state, when restored from his banishment, by this word. (*Cic. ad Attic. lib.* vi. *Epist.* 6.)

The *Greeks* expressed by it *the doctrine of the Brahmans*, in which they affirmed our entering on *a new state of being* after death. (*Clem. Alex. Strom. lib.* iii. *pag.* 451.) And the *Stoics* used it to denote their expected *renovation of the world* after successive conflagrations. (*Marc. Antonin. Medit. lib.* xi. § I. v. 13, x. 7. See *Lucian, Oper. pag.* 532. *Euseb. Præp: Evang. ex numen. lib.* xv. *chap.* 19. *Phil. Jud. de Mundi Immort. pag.* 940, 951, and in many other places.) And so *the fathers* often use it to signify *the resurrection* which Christians expect. (*See Euseb. Eccl. Hist. lib.* v. *chap.* I. *in fin.*) Compare *Matt.* xix. 28, and the *Note* there: *Fam. Expos. Vol.* II. *pag.* 238.

versy is laid; but on considering them attentively, I find nothing in either of them to lead us to think *baptism* the regeneration spoken of there.

As to the former of them, *John* iii. 5, when our Lord says, *Except a man be born of water, and of the Spirit, he can not enter into the kingdom of GOD;* it is (after all the contempt with which that interpretation has been treated) very possible he may mean, by a well-known figure, to express *one idea* by both those clauses, that is, *the purifying influences of the Spirit* cleansing the mind, as *water* does the body: as elsewhere, to be *baptized with the Holy Ghost and with fire*, (*Matt.* iii. 11,) signifies to be baptized *by the Spirit* operating *like fire*. But if there is indeed a *reference to baptism* in these words (which I own I am much inclined to believe) it will by no means follow that *baptism* is REGENERATION. On that supposition, I still think the sense of the passage must be that which I have given in my *paraphrase* on it (*Fam. Expos. vol. I. p.* 148—*p.* 57 *Am. Ed.*) "Whosoever would become a regular member of the kingdom of GOD, must not only be baptized, but as ever he desires to share in its spiritual and eternal blessings, must experience the renewing and sanctifying influences of the Holy Spirit on his soul, to cleanse it from the power of corruption, and to animate and quicken it to a spiritual and Divine life." It is granted therefore, that how excellent soever any man's character is, he must be *baptized* before he can be looked upon as completely *a member* of the church of Christ; and that, in general, *being born of the Spirit,* he will also be solicitous that he may *be born of water*, and so *fulfill all righteousness.* But it will never follow from hence, that *being born of water* and *born of the Spirit* are the same thing. The text rather implies they are *different*; and I think every body must own, they may be *actually separate.*

Nothing therefore can be more absurd than to infer from this text, that if there be two persons, one of whom is *born of the Spirit*, and *not of water;* another *of water*, and *not of the Spirit;* the latter, that is, *the wicked man*, who has perhaps with some iniquitous design been *baptized*, may properly be said to be *regenerated*, or born of *GOD*, and consequently to be *an heir of GOD*, (*Rom.* viii. 17,) rather than a *truly religious man* who has *not yet been baptized*, either through want of opportunity, or through some unhappy mistake, as to the nature and design, or the perpetuity and obligations of that ordinance. Now this I take to be *precisely the question*, and must declare that when *a baptized person* is destitute of true religion, *that birth* which he had *by water*, seems to me as it were *an evanescent thing*, or a thing which disappears as unworthy the mention; and that it must be therefore most safe and advisable, as well as most agreeable to the scripture sense, to appropriate the title of *regenerate persons* to those *sanctified by Divine grace*, rather than to use it of *all who are baptized.*

As to the text in *Titus* (*chap.* iii. 5,) where God is said to *save us by the washing of regeneration*, or, as some earnestly contend it should be rendered, *by the laver of regeneration:* I might answer, that as that interpretation is by no means necessary,* it cannot be proved that *baptism* is here designed; though I acknowledge there may be a graceful allusion to it. The *Apostle* may mean, we are saved *by GOD'S washing our hearts by his* sanctifying *Spirit* (a phrase so often used in the *Old Testament*) and thereby *making us his child-*

* The original is δια λουτρου παλιγγενεσιας. Now it is certain *the seventy* use another word, that is Λουτηρ, to signify *Laver, Exod.* xxx. 18, 28; xxxi. 9; and I think (so far as I have observed) everywhere else: and Λουτρον (*St. Paul's* word here) is used where it can not signify *laver*, for *the water in which sheep are washed, Cant.* iv. 2, and for a *large quantity of water* in which an adult person was *washed* or *bathed. Eph.* v. 26. And this remark quite overthrows all the argument from *this text*, if any argument would follow from rendering it *laver:* but I think I need not urge this.

ren: and in this sense it might have been used, though *baptism* had never been instituted. But granting (as I have done) that Λουτρον may be rendered *laver*, and that *baptism* may be the *laver* referred to; and that "there is indeed an allusion to the *washing new-born children;* (as *Mr. Mede* in his *diatribe* on this text contends;) I think this text will be so far from proving that *St. Paul* meant to call *baptism* REGENERATION, that it will prove the contrary: for *regeneration* itself, *and the laver of regeneration*, can not be the same thing. And whatever *Tertullian* and other ancients may fancifully talk of our being *generated like fishes in the water*, in a weak allusion to the technical word ΙΧΘΥΣ, (a fish,) common sense will see how absurd it would be to apply this to a *child*, and will teach us rather to argue, that as *children* must be *born* before they can be *washed*, so they must be *regenerated* before *the washiug of regeneration* (that is, the washing which belongs to their new birth,) can be applied to them. But on the whole, I am more and more inclined to think there is *no reference* at all here *to a laver*, or to the *washing new-born children;* and therefore, that this *washing* and *the renewing of the Holy Ghost* are exegetical, and that the latter clause might be rendered, *even the renewing, &c.*, which makes the text decisive for the sense in which I use the word.

After all, then, if any argument can be deduced from *scripture* in favor of the manner of speaking now in debate, it must be from *the general tenor of it;* according to which it seems that all who are *members of the visible church* are spoken of as *regenerate;* from which it may be inferred, with some plausible probability at least, that *baptism*, by which they are admitted into that society, may be called Regeneration. And I am ready to believe, as I hinted above, that this was the chief reason why *the ancients* so often used the word in the sense I am now opposing.

Now with relation to this, I desire it may be recollected, that when Christianity first appeared in the world, it was attended with such discouragements, as made the very *profession of it*, in a great measure, *a test of men's characters.* The Apostles therefore, knowing the number of hypocrites to be comparatively very small, generally take no notice of them, but address themselves to *whole bodies of Christians*, as if they were truly what they professed to be. Just as our *Lord Jesus Christ*, though he knew the wickedness of *Judas*, often addressed himself to the *whole body* of his *Apostles*, as if they were *all* his faithful servants, and makes gracious declarations and promises to the *whole society*, which could by no means be applicable to this one corrupt and wretched member of it; telling them, for instance, that *they should* share in his final triumph, and *sit on twelve thrones, judging the twelve tribes of Israel. Matt.* xix. 28.

THIS is therefore *the true key* to all those passages in which *Christians* are, *in the general*, said to be *adopted, sanctified, justified, &c.*, as well as *regenerated.* The *Apostles* had reason, in the judgment of charity, to think thus of by far the greatest part of them; and therefore they *speak to them all*, as in such a happy state. And agreeably to this, we find not only *such privileges*, but also *such characters*, ascribed to *Christians in general*, as were only applicable to such of them as were *Christians indeed.* Thus all the *Corinthians* are spoken of by the Apostle *Paul*, as *waiting for the coming of our Lord Jesus Christ*, (1 *Cor.* i. 7,) and all the *Ephesians*, and all the *Colossians*, as having *faith in the Lord Jesus Christ, and love to all the saints*, (*Eph.* i. 15; *Col.* i. 4,) and all the *Philippians*, as having a *good work begun in them*, which *Paul* was persuaded *GOD would perfect*, (*Phil.* i. 6,) and all the *Thessalonians*, as remarkable for *their work of faith, and labor of love, and patience of hope;* (1 *Thess.* i. 3;) though it evidently appears there were persons in several of these churches who behaved much amiss, and to whom, had he been particularly addressing each of them alone, he could not by any means have used such language. On the like principles *Peter*, when addressing all the *Christians* in *Pontus*, *Galatia*, *Cappadocia*, *Asia*, and *Bithynia*, speaks of the whole aggregate of them, (1 *Pet.* i. 8,) as *loving an unseen Saviour*, and amidst all their tribulations, *rejoicing in him with joy unspeakable and full of glory;* though probably there were some *weak* and *dejected Christians* among them, and undoubtedly in so large an extent of country, in which there were such a vast number of churches, *not a few*, who (as *our Lord* afterwards expresses it of some of them) *had only a name to live, while they were dead;* (*Rev.* iii. 1 :) in which passage, by the way, *our Lord* uses the same figure, and describes *the whole body* by the character of those who made the greater of it.

I STATE the matter thus particularly, because I think this obvious remark is a sufficient answer to what is most peculiar and important in a late Discourse, consisting of near 130 *quarto pages*, and entitled *A Key to the Apostolic Writings, &c.*, prefixed by the Rev. Mr. *Taylor*, of *Norwich*, to his late *Paraphrase* and *Notes* on the

*Romans.** I think what I have briefly advanced here, will much more effectually answer the end of fixing *the true sense* of the *scripture phrases* in question. And I cannot forbear saying, that to determine the sense of the words *called, redeemed, sanctified, &c.*, when applied to the *Christian church*, by that in which they are used in *Moses* and *the prophets* with respect to *the whole people of Israel*, seems to me as unreasonable, as it would be to maintain, that the dimensions, the strength, and the beauty of a body are to be most exactly estimated by looking on its shadow.

YET on this evidently weak and mistaken principle, the learned and ingenious Author referred to above, ventures not only to attempt *an entire alteration* in the generally-received strain of theological Discourses, but to throw out a censure, which, considering its extent and its severity, must either be very terrible, or very pitiable. He not only seems to think, if I understand him right, that we were *all regenerated* (if at all) as well as *justified*, in those of *our parents* who were *first converted* from *idolatry* to *Christianity*, (*Key*, § 81, 82, and 246,) as indeed he expressly says, "that we are *born* in a *justified*," and therefore

* And with singular inconsistency adopted by Dr. Adam Clarke, in his Commentary on the New Testament, now so widely circulated.—J. N. B.

undoubtedly, (if the word is to be retained,) in *a regenerate* "state:" but he presumes to say, that *such doctrines* as have been almost universally taught and received among *Christians*, concerning "*Justification, regeneration, redemption, &c.*, have quite taken away the very ground of the Christian life, the *grace* of GOD, and have left no object for the faith of a sinner to work upon." (§ 357.) And hereupon, lest it should be forgot, he repeats it in the *same section*, that to represent it as "the subject of doubtful inquiry, trial, and examination, whether we have *an interest in Christ*, whether we are *in a state of pardon*, whether we be *adopted*, (and by consequence, to be sure, whether we be *regenerated*,) "is" (as the *Antinomians* I imagine would also say,) "to make *our justification*, as it invests us in those blessings, to be of *works*, and not by faith alone;" and (as we just before said in the same words,) "to take away the very ground of the Christian life, the *grace* of GOD, and to leave no object for the faith of a sinner to act upon." And *this way of stating things*, which has so generally prevailed, is joined with the *wickedness* and *contentions* of professing *Christians*, as a third *cause* of that *disregard to the Gospel* which is so common in the present day.

Now as no book can fall more directly under

this censure, than this of *mine*, in which, it is the business of the first three discourses to direct professing Christians into an *inquiry*, whether they be or be not in a *regenerate state;* I thought it not improper, in this *postscript*, briefly to acquaint my reader with the principles on which I continue to think *the view*, in which I have put the matter, to be *rational* and *scriptural*,* and do still in my conscience judge it *far*

* For the full proof of this, that it is *the most scriptural sense*, I must desire the reader diligently to examine, and seriously to consider, *the several texts* which are quoted in the foregoing Discourses.

Let it still be remembered, that to be *regenerated*, and to be *born of GOD*, are *equivalent phrases:* And with this remark, let any one that can do it *paraphrase* all the passages referred to, in two different views; first putting the word *baptism* for *regeneration*, and *baptized persons* for *born of GOD;* and then substituting *our definition of regeneration* or of *a regenerate person*, instead of the *words themselves:* and I can not but think he will be struck with *that demonstration*, which will (as it were) emerge of itself upon such a trial. And I must add, that if he looks into *the context* of many of these passages, he will at the same time see how utterly ungrounded it is to assert, as some have done, "that *regeneration* is only used when applied to *Jewish converts to Christianity*, referring to their *former birth from Abraham;*" a notion so fully confuted by *our Lord's discourse with Nicodemus, John* iii. 3, *et seq.* by *Tit.* iii. 5, and by 1 *Pet.* i. 3, 23; ii. 2, when compared with 1 *Pet.* i. 14: iv. 3, (which proves that the *Apostle* there wrote to societies, of which the greater part had before been *idolatrous Gentiles.*)

preferable to what *the advocates of baptismal regeneration* on the one hand, or *Dr. Taylor* on the other, would introduce.

It seems to me, that the points in dispute with *him* are much more important than our debates with *them*, as a much greater number of *Scriptures* are concerned, and the whole tenor of our *ministerial addresses* would be much more sensibly affected. Had I leisure to discuss the matter more largely with this gentleman, I should think it might be an important service to the *Gospel of Christ*. I hope it will be undertaken by some abler hand; and shall, in the mean time, go on *preaching* and *writing* in the manner so solemnly condemned, with no apprehension from the discharge of all this *overloaded artillery*, except it be what I feel for the zealous engineer himself, and a few other friends who may chance to stand nearer him than in prudence they ought.

P. D.

Northampton, June 13, 1745.

www.ingramcontent.com/pod-product-compliance
Lightning Source LLC
LaVergne TN
LVHW010207110826
845151LV00002B/632

* 9 7 8 1 4 2 5 5 3 5 5 0 6 *